Collins

Key S...

Ge...
En...

Book 1

David Weath...
Nicholas Sh...
Rebecca Kit...

07/21

D1512776

This book should be returned/renewed by the latest date shown above. Overdue items incur charges which prevent self-service renewals. Please contact the library.

Wandsworth Libraries
24 hour Renewal Hotline
01159 293388
www.wandsworth.gov.uk

THE BRIGHTER BOROUGH
Wandsworth

9030 00007 4865 2

William Collins' dream of knowledge for all began with the publication of his first book in 1819. A self-educated mill worker, he not only enriched millions of lives, but also founded a flourishing publishing house. Today, staying true to this spirit, Collins books are packed with inspiration, innovation and practical expertise. They place you at the centre of a world of possibility and give you exactly what you need to explore it.

Collins. Freedom to teach

Published by Collins
An imprint of HarperCollins*Publishers* Ltd
Westerhill Road
Bishopbriggs
Glasgow G64 2QT
www.harpercollins.co.uk

Collins® is a registered trademark of HarperCollins*Publisher*

Browse the complete Collins catalogue at www.collinseduca

First edition 2014
© HarperCollins*Publishers* Limited 2014
Maps © Collins Bartholomew Ltd 2014

10 9 8 7

ISBN 978-0-00-741103-0

LONDON BOROUGH OF WANDSWORTH	
9030 00007 4865 2	
Askews & Holts	
J910 JUNIOR NON-FICT	
	WW21002354

David Weatherly, Nicholas Sheehan and Rebecca Kitchen assert their moral rights to be identified as the authors of this work

All rights reserved. No part of this publication may be reproduced, stored in a retrieval system, or transmitted, in any form or by any means, electronic, mechanical, photocopying, recording or otherwise without the prior permission in writing of the publisher and copyright owners.

The contents of this publication are believed correct at the time of printing. Nevertheless the publisher can accept no responsibility for errors or omissions, changes in the detail given or for any expense or loss thereby caused.

HarperCollins does not warrant that any website mentioned in this title will be provided uninterrupted, that any website will be error free, that defects will be corrected, or that the website or the server that makes it available are free of viruses or bugs. For full terms and conditions please refer to the site terms provided on the website.

A catalogue record for this book is available from the British Library

Typeset, designed, edited and proofread by Palimpsest Book Production Ltd, Falkirk, Stirlingshire
Cover designs by Angela English

Printed and bound by CPI Group (UK) Ltd, Croydon CR0 4YY

The mapping in this publication is generated from Collins Bartholomew digital databases.
Collins Bartholomew, the UK's leading independent geographical information supplier, can provide a digital, custom, and premium mapping service to a variety of markets.
For further information:
Tel: +44 (0) 208 307 4593
e-mail: collinsbartholomew@harpercollins.co.uk

Visit our websites at: www.collins.co.uk or www.collinsbartholomew.com

If you would like to comment on any aspect of this book, please contact us at the above address or online.
e-mail: collinsmaps@harpercollins.co.uk

Contents

About this book

Why is seeing the world today as a geographer so important?

This is Noah. He's just a week or so old. There's a chance that he might be the first person in the world to live to be 150 years old. He will almost certainly live to see the next century.

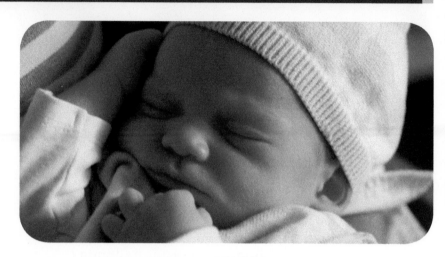

In Noah's lifetime, how is the world going to change and what opportunities and challenges will he encounter? It's impossible to predict of course, but it is worth pausing for a moment to consider what the world was like eighty or so years ago. The use of antibiotics in medicine was in its infancy. There were no jet engines, satellites, nuclear power reactors or even ball point pens! Space travel was still confined to science fiction novels. In 1935, the world's population stood at 2.2 billion. Since then an extra five billion people have been added.

No one can predict the future but what we do know is that there are challenges ahead. It is likely that there will be eleven billion people on the planet by 2100. How are all these people going to be adequately fed, housed and cared for medically? How will economic development and sustainability be balanced so as to provide everyone with a comfortable lifestyle that doesn't impact negatively, either on other people elsewhere in the world or the environment which supports us all?

The Environment Agency in Britain anticipates that here there could be almost a one metre increase in relative sea levels by the end of the century, combined with an average temperature increase of 0.2 °C per decade and a 0.5 m rise in the height of storm surges. Decisions need to be made now about the best way to manage these situations and other impacts of climate change, such as the emergence of **environmental refugees**.

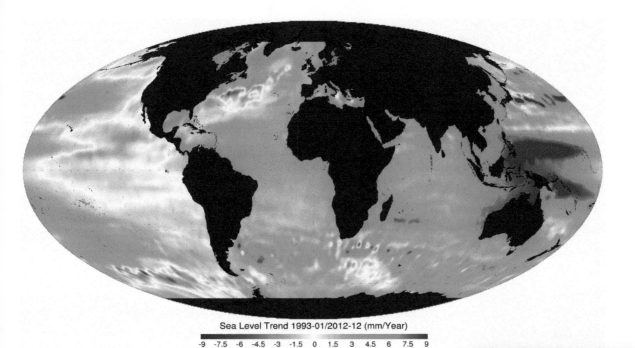

Sea Level Trend 1993-01/2012-12 (mm/Year)

-9 -7.5 -6 -4.5 -3 -1.5 0 1.5 3 4.5 6 7.5 9

The *New York Times* recently reported that in Bangladesh, storms, flooding and crop damage from rising sea levels are forcing people out of their villages at a rate of 400,000 a year. Most move to Dhaka, which is itself only a few metres above sea level and regularly hit by cyclones and floods, and is one of the world's megacities most vulnerable to the effects of global warming.

In Alaska, melting **permafrost** and increased levels of coastal erosion are creating America's first climate refugees. Watch the film at http://www.theguardian.com/environment/interactive/2013/may/13/newtok-alaska-climate-change-refugees.

Geographers see the links and relationships between the environments that surround us and the way in which we live our lives. They understand how people and environments interact and as a result are ideally placed for coming up with ideas and plans for tackling big issues. Not surprisingly therefore, we think that learning about the world and the challenges which face it and coming up with possible solutions through studying geography is really important – amongst the most important things you can do at school, in fact! We want you to be not only really good at geography but also to become a good geographer; someone who can make connections and apply what you have learned in one place to situations you encounter elsewhere.

'The study of geography is about more than just memorizing places on a map. It's about understanding the complexity of our world and in the end, it's about using all that knowledge to help bridge divides and bring people together.'

US President Barack Obama, 2012

'So many of the world's current issues – at a global scale and locally – boil down to geography, and we need the geographers of the future to help us understand them.'

Michael Palin, 2013

In this book we introduce you to the kind of geographical issues and challenges that are relevant to the world in which you live, now and in the future. So, you will find topics about: coping with and managing **natural hazards**; why some countries are 'buying' other countries; how best to secure our energy supplies in the future; the impact of living in places with very high population densities; and the reasoning behind where major global sporting events end up being located. Oh, and we also want you to consider why an event which happened over 250 million years ago still has a major effect on our lives today. You still get to learn about lots of countries and places in the world and everything links with the knowledge and understanding required by the National Curriculum.

The way in which we want you to learn is very important too. Each of the seven topics is a geographical enquiry with a big question to answer through a process of investigation carried out by you. We have organised each enquiry so that, through a number of stages, you come to know and understand the topic under consideration really well. We then support you to apply that knowledge. Learning activities running through each investigation encourage you to make those crucial people–environment links, make judgements, evaluate situations and reach decisions as a geographer rather than someone who is just good at geography.

There are resources and information in the Teacher Book to assist you as well. At regular intervals during the enquiries we pause to enable you to consolidate your thinking before moving on and from time to time there are opportunities to extend your enquiry in different directions if you wish. Each of the enquiries has an outcome for you to produce but they are not all written pieces. Some involve practical work and model-making, whilst others are ICT based.

Above all, we really hope that working through these enquiries with your teacher will contribute to developing a lifelong love of the subject and the wonder of the world in which we live. There are certainly many geographical challenges to be faced in the years ahead but there are also an equal number of opportunities to be grasped. Managing those challenges and realising the opportunities for the benefit of Noah and all who live on the planet is going to require geographers – people such as yourselves, who understand how people interact with their environments and who are able to contribute in an informed way to making decisions about the most sustainable way forward for us all.

David Weatherly | Nicholas Sheehan | Rebecca Kitchen

Where in the world will your enquiries take you?

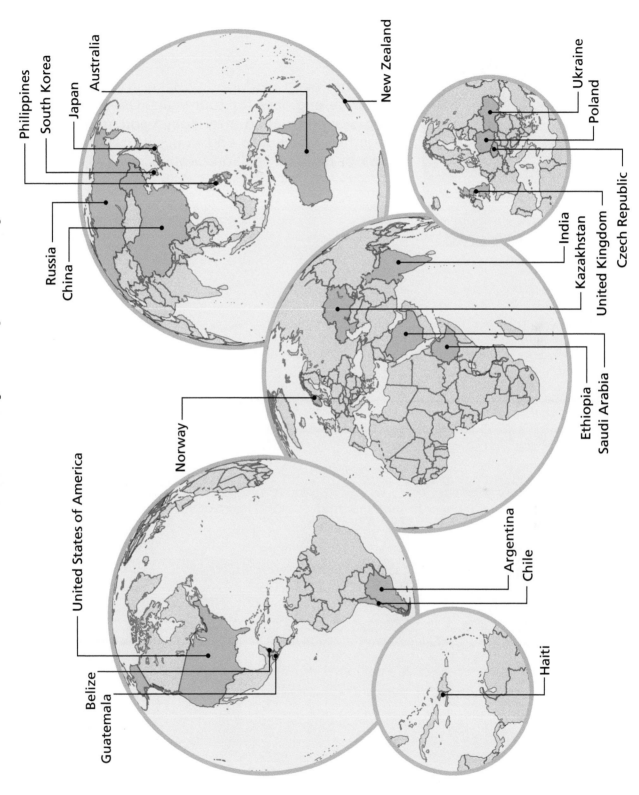

Philippines
South Korea
Japan
Australia
New Zealand

Russia
China

Ukraine
Poland
Czech Republic

India
Kazakhstan
United Kingdom

Norway

Ethiopia
Saudi Arabia

United States of America

Argentina
Chile

Belize
Guatemala

Haiti

1 Living in Japan

Why isn't Yuna able to play the sport she loves?

Yuna has been working in Osaka in Japan as a software engineer for four years. Osaka is the third-largest city in Japan after Tokyo and Yokohama and together with Kyoto and Kobe forms a **metropolitan area** of nineteen million people.

Asia

RUSSIA

CYPRUS
LEBANON
ISRAEL
JORDAN
TURKEY
GEORGIA
SYRIA
IRAQ
AZER.
KAZAKHSTAN
MONGOLIA
IRAN
KUWAIT
BAHRAIN
QATAR
U.A.E.
SAUDI
ARABIA
YEMEN
OMAN
TURKMENISTAN
UZBEKISTAN
AFGHANISTAN
PAKISTAN
TAJIKISTAN
KYRGYZSTAN
CHINA
N. KOREA
S. KOREA
JAPAN
INDIA
NEPAL
BHUTAN
BANGLADESH
MYANMAR
(BURMA)
LAOS
THAILAND
VIETNAM
CAMBODIA
SRI LANKA
MALAYSIA
SINGAPORE
BRUNEI
PHILIPPINES
TAIWAN
INDONESIA
EAST TIMOR

Sea of
Okhotsk
Ostrov
Kunashir

PACIFIC
OCEAN

JAPAN

Sea of Japan
(East Sea)

Hokkaidō

Wakkanai
Kitami
Asahikawa
Asahi-dake
2290
Obihiro
Kushiro
Otaru
Sapporo
Tomakomai
Muroran
Samani
Mori
Hakodate
Tsugaru-kaikyo

Aomori
Hachinohe
Hirosaki
Miyako
Noshiro
Morioka
Akita
Kamaishi
Ichinoseki
Sakata
Ishinomaki
Yamagata
Sendai
Sadoga-shima
Niigata
Fukushima
Aizu-wakamatsu
Kōriyama
Kashiwazaki
Nagaoka
Iwaki
Jōetsu
Utsunomiya
Hitachi
Toyama
Nagano
Maebashi
Mito
Kanazawa
Yariga-take
3180
Ueda
Ōyama
Tsuchiura
Komatsu
Matsumoto
Saitama
Sakura
Fukui
Shirane-san
3192
Kōfu
Fuji-san
3776
Tōkyō
Chiba
Kawasaki
Yokohama
Numazu
Shizuoka
O-shima

Oki-shotō
Maizuru
Ogaki
Gifu
Nagoya
Tottori
Toyota
Matsue
Kyōto
Suzuka
Hamamatsu
Ōsaka
Tsu
Okayama
Matsusaka
Kōbe
Sakai
Ise
Takamatsu
Wakayama
Hiroshima
Seto-naiko
Tokushima
Kii-suidō
Shimonoseki
Matsuyama
Kōchi
Tsushima
Shikoku
Higashi-suidō
Iki
Kita-Kyūshū
Fukuoka
Kurume
Kuju-san
1788
Sasebo
Kumamoto
Nagasaki
Kyūshū
Miyazaki
Kagoshima

Honshū

Elevation
3000 – 5000 m
2000 – 3000 m
1000 – 2000 m
500 – 1000 m
200 – 500 m
0 – 200 m

— Road
— Railway
⊛ Airport
▣ Capital city

Wakasa-
wan
Tottori
Maizuru
Ōgaki
Gifu
Biwa-ko
Nagoya
Kyōto
Honshū
Okayama
Kōbe
Ōsaka
Suzuka
Takamatsu
Sakai
Tsu
Matsusaka
Tokushima
Wakayama
Ise
Shikoku
Kii-suidō

Yuna shares a rented **condominium** in the city with two friends. She joined a software design company straight from university and at 27 years old is currently earning US$39,000 a year. She enjoys her work but the hours can be very long – sometimes up to fifty hours a week.

Yuna also finds that being a software engineer can be highly pressurised, particularly in the run up to meeting tight deadlines for clients. The one thing that Yuna finds can really help with the stress, as well as keeping her fit, is to play tennis. She has always loved tennis, right from the very first time she played it at school. Now, although she has the time in the evenings and at the weekend, she doesn't get to play much.

Look at the images of **urban** Japan.

What clues are there here to help explain why Yuna finds playing tennis difficult even though she has the time?

Make a list of possible reasons.

What is the connection between lack of living space and the price of available land?

What do you think the law of supply and demand means?

The key reason that Yuna isn't playing the sport she loves is that playing tennis at clubs and centres throughout Japan is very expensive. At the Utsobo Park Tennis Club in Osaka where Yuna likes to play, each player has to pay US$26 an hour for a court. Yuna finds that even though she is earning a decent salary this is too expensive for her to play very often.

A two-hour game plus the cost of travel to and from her home in Ikuno-Ku is well over US$78. In fact, tennis is not the only sport that is expensive in Japan. For example, if Yuna's passion were golf then she would have exactly the same challenge.

At the semi-public golf courses in Japan it is possible to play for US$78 but many courses charge much more than this. In fact, many Japanese golfers find it cheaper to fly to Hawaii or Thailand to play golf than to do so at home. Japanese investors have financed numerous golf courses in Malaysia, Indonesia, Hawaii, Thailand and Singapore to cater for Japanese golfers who can't afford to play regularly at home.

1.2 So why is playing sports such as tennis and golf so expensive in Japan?

Three-quarters of the land area of Japan is mountainous. With a population of 128 million, this means that **population density** is generally very high (the average for the whole country is 336 people per km^2) but this rises to 5500 per km^2 in parts of the Tokyo-Yokohama **megalopolis** along the east coast of the island of Honshu, where thirty-five million people live.

As a result, flat land for building, farming and providing sports facilities is in short supply. Because land that can be developed is scarce, its price rises: this is the law of supply and demand. Figures from www.globalpropertyguide.com show that during 2013, the average price of land in the Osaka Metropolitan Area, where Yuna lives, increased by 2.3% to US$1287 per m^2. The average price of a new two-roomed condominium in Osaka is now US$5283 per m^2. It is not uncommon for a two-roomed condominium in Osaka to cost over US$840,000.

Take a look at the range of properties on offer in Osaka at:

http://www.century21 global.com

- Of the available condominiums in Osaka, what is the cheapest per square metre rate available?

- How does location within Osaka affect prices?

- What is the connection or relationship between these three images?

- Using the **relief** map on page 9, what proportion of the land area of Japan would you estimate as being below 200 m and above 500 m?

- What is the correlation (or link) between where most people in Japan live and the relief of the land?

- In terms of the proportion of land covered, what is the most important **land use** in Japan? Why do you think this?

- Considered together, what evidence do these factors provide to help explain why Yuna finds it difficult to play tennis?

▶▶

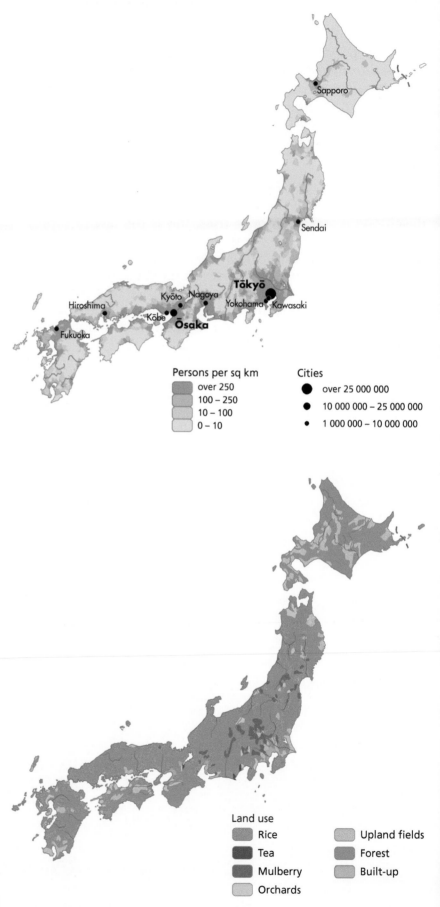

Persons per sq km
- over 250
- 100 – 250
- 10 – 100
- 0 – 10

Cities
- ● over 25 000 000
- ● 10 000 000 – 25 000 000
- • 1 000 000 – 10 000 000

Land use
- Rice
- Tea
- Mulberry
- Orchards
- Upland fields
- Forest
- Built-up

Night-time satellite image of Japan

The Japanese archipelago (island chain) consists of four main islands – Honshu, Shikoku, Kyushu and Hokkaido – together with thousands of surrounding smaller ones. Most of the Japanese mountains are covered with dense forest. Only 15% of the land area of Japan is suitable for use either as farmland or living space and consequently agricultural and urban areas are concentrated together.

With a relatively large population of 128 million, the people of Japan have learned to adapt their patterns of living to become better suited to the environment in which they live.

▶ Consolidating your thinking ◀

Look at the following images of urban and mountainous areas of the prefecture of Osaka in which Yuna lives. How do they show the people's **adaptation** to a lack of living space? Make a list of all the ways in which people have had to modify or redesign the way they live and earn a living.

How does all of this affect Yuna? Read through all of the information cards (which can be printed from pages 8–11 of the Teacher Book) and then sort them into sets to provide you with information about:

- The physical geography of Japan
- The impact of physical geography on **population distribution** and density in Japan
- Yuna
- Osaka
- Utsobo Tennis Club

Be sure to use appropriate subject vocabulary throughout your narrative e.g. **relief; urban; megalopolis; population density/distribution; coastal** etc.

Next you need to draft a piece of explanatory writing to bring all of this information together and help you answer the key question at the beginning of this enquiry. Use the information you have categorised above, plus additional reading of your own (additional sources are recommended below) to demonstrate that you understand the geographical reasons which explain why Yuna isn't able to play very much of the sport she loves. Your explanatory narrative needs to have the following structure:

- **A Title:** Why can't Yuna play the sport she loves?

- **An introductory paragraph** to set the scene and context – in this case providing background information on Yuna, where she lives and the life she leads. You will need to consider whether you will use maps and images to help set the context.

- **A second paragraph**, which begins with a **topic sentence** (this introduces the reader to what the paragraph is going to be about). In this paragraph you will discuss the **physical geography** of Japan and link this with appropriate maps and images.

- **A third paragraph** (the focus of which will again be introduced via a topic sentence), which explains the impact of the physical geography of Japan on human activity (e.g. where and how people are able to live) using connectives such as 'since', 'because', 'so', 'as', 'therefore' and then 'this leads to', 'which causes', 'this means', 'as a result of', 'due to the fact that', etc.

- **A concluding paragraph**, which is a summary of the main points and answers the question. Once again, look to apply appropriate connectives such as 'in conclusion', 'in summary', 'to sum up', 'overall', 'on the whole', 'in short', 'in brief', 'to conclude', 'so to round off', etc.

A model of explanatory writing, which provides the same kind of structure as the piece that you are going to write about Yuna, and which illustrates the key conventions, is available for you to print off from the Teacher Book (pp.12–13). Read through this example carefully and use it as the basis for your explanation of: *Why can't Yuna play the sport she loves?*

Use the additional sources of information to the right to extend the depth and breadth of your explanation.

During the drafting stage of this piece of explanatory writing why not swap your developing answer with a partner and each use the table in the Teacher Book (p.14) to check how your respective answers are shaping up? Discuss with your partner which aspects of your explanatory writing you feel are most effective so far and which require further development.

Useful general background on factors affecting population distribution:

http://www.sln.org.uk/ geography/schools/ blythebridge/GCSERevision PopulationD&D.htm

http://www.bbc.co.uk/schools/ gcsebitesize/geography/ population/population_ distribution_rev1.shtml

http://www.bbc.co.uk/ learningzone/clips/ population-density-and- distribution/532.html

More specific to Japan:

http://www.countrystudies.us/ japan/51.htm

http://www.shmslevasseur. files.wordpress.com/2009/08/ chapter-31.pdf

http://www.afe.easia. columbia.edu/japan/ japanworkbook/geography/ japgeo.html

Extending your enquiry 》

1.3 How is Japan creating more living space through *umetatechi*?

Because living space is in such short supply, the people of Japan have been reclaiming land from the sea for nearly 1000 years – the first man-made island of Kyogashima was created in 1173. The first large-scale reclamation project was started in Tokyo Bay in 1592. Today, 0.5% of the entire land area of Japan is estimated to be made of **reclaimed land** or *umetatechi*.

▶ Consolidating your thinking ◀

Look carefully at the images of Tokyo Bay on the following page. The map dates from 1898. How has the coastline changed since then? What shape are the land extensions and islands that have been created in Tokyo Bay over the years? Look at the map on this page, in which decade did most land reclamation in Tokyo Bay occur? Why do you think this was? How is the reclaimed land being used today?

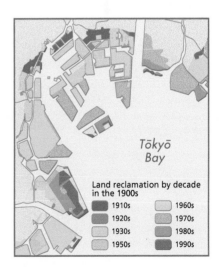

Tōkyō Bay

Land reclamation by decade in the 1900s

■ 1910s	■ 1960s
■ 1920s	■ 1970s
■ 1930s	■ 1980s
■ 1950s	■ 1990s

Map of Tokyo Bay in the 1890s

Aerial photo of Tokyo Bay today

Read the notes on the lack of living space in urban Japan on p.15 to extend your understanding of this problem.

There are several stages in the process of reclaiming land from inter-tidal areas around the coast. Like Japan, the Netherlands in Europe has a very long history of reclaiming land in order to increase its living space. Here, the areas of new land are called **polders**. Spend some time researching the process of reclaiming land in both of these countries.

The new Kansai International Airport opened in 1994 and is built on an artificial island in the middle of Osaka Bay, twenty-four miles from Osaka City. It currently handles fourteen million passengers each year. Originally, the new airport was planned to be built on the mainland near Kobe but the city refused the plan. The existing Osaka International Airport could not be expanded because it was surrounded by densely populated suburbs.

Construction started in 1987. The sea wall was finished in 1989 and is made of rock and 48,000 tetrahedral concrete blocks. Three mountains were excavated to produce twenty-one million cubic metres (twenty-seven million cubic yards) of landfill. It took 10,000 workers and ten million work hours over three years, using eighty ships, to complete the thirty-metre (98 ft) layer of earth over the sea floor and inside the sea wall.

In 1990, a three-kilometre bridge (carrying road and rail links) was completed to connect the island to the mainland at Rinku Town, at a cost of US$1 billion. A second runway was added in 2007, allowing the airport to operate twenty-four hours a day. Over 15,000 people are employed at the airport and in economic activities on the mainland that are linked to it.

Kansai International Airport under construction

Produce an annotated flow diagram on a piece of A3 plain paper that explains the technology and engineering used to create new land from the sea.

- Examine all of the resources again and make a list of two columns: costs and benefits.

- Who or what do you think might have benefited from the construction of the airport and who or what might have been placed at a disadvantage?

- The map opposite will help you to think about the position of some key stakeholders. A stakeholder is anyone with an interest in a development, event or business and can include individuals, groups or organisations that are affected by the planned activity.

- How and why might each of these stakeholders have welcomed or been concerned about the construction of the airport?

- Discuss your views with others and draw up a list that everyone has had a chance to contribute to.

▶▶

Not without controversy

Whilst the airport was an amazing piece of engineering, which needed to be designed to withstand earthquakes, typhoons and their associated tidal surges, it was not universally welcomed by everyone.

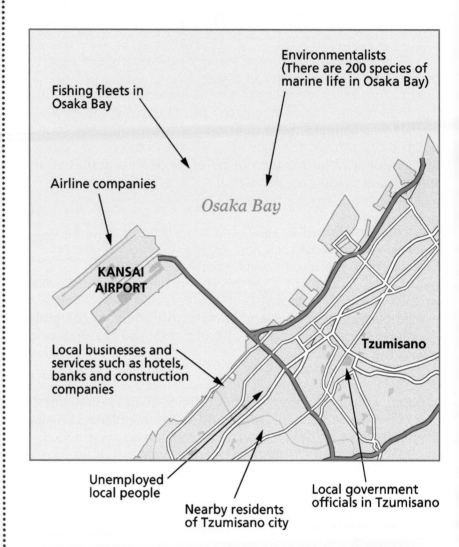

Environmentalists (There are 200 species of marine life in Osaka Bay)

Fishing fleets in Osaka Bay

Airline companies

Osaka Bay

KANSAI AIRPORT

Tzumisano

Local businesses and services such as hotels, banks and construction companies

Unemployed local people

Nearby residents of Tzumisano city

Local government officials in Tzumisano

An eco-airport in Osaka Bay?

From the time of its design and construction the operators of Kansai International Airport have been following an **Environmental Management Plan** based on the principles of **sustainable development** to create what they hope will be an example of an eco-airport in Osaka Bay. According to one definition, sustainable development demands that we seek ways of living and working that enable all people of the world to lead healthy, fulfilling and economically secure lives without impacting negatively on the environment and without endangering the future welfare of all the people on the planet.

The Kansai International Airport Environmental Management Plan can be found at http://www.nkiac.co.jp/en/env/index.html#smartisland. The plan is based on the principles that Kansai would be an airport which:

• protects a pleasant regional environment

• has a low impact on the global environment

• recycles

• values nature

• exists in harmony with the social community.

- • Read through the plan carefully.

- • The management board of the airport set performance targets for each of the principles of the plan. How does the airport measure up in terms of meeting its targets?

- • In what ways is the airport addressing the needs and concerns of local stakeholders?

- • Are there any stakeholders' issues that were raised during your discussion that you think are not being addressed through the plan? If so, what do you feel could be done by the airport authorities?

- • Overall, do you feel that Kansai International Airport can be considered as a case study of sustainable development according to the definition quoted above?

Japan is not the only country in the world in which pressure on available land from a wide variety of **residential**, **commercial** and **recreational** interests has led to reclamation from the sea in order to create more living space. For example, over 25% of the territory of Hong Kong is now reclaimed land. Most of the urban areas of Hong Kong have been built on reclaimed land (shown in red on the map).

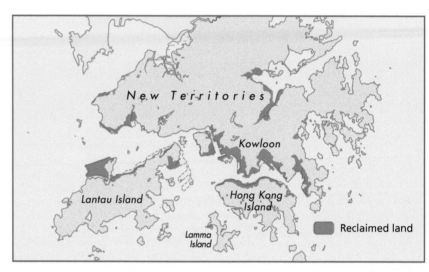

With a population of sixty-one million people and an average population density of 262 people per km² (compared with 336 per km² in Japan), the United Kingdom also faces the challenge of a lack of living space in parts of the country (such as the Southeast where population density averages 452 per km²). Finding space for activities requiring very large areas of land is particularly problematic and often highly controversial. Building or expanding an airport is one such activity.

In the United Kingdom, the two runways of London's Heathrow Airport handle over seventy million passengers each year, travelling with eighty-four airlines to and from eighty countries through five terminals, making it the busiest airport in the world. A third of passengers transfer to other flights, which means it is also a major hub airport. The growth of air traffic over the last twenty years has meant that Heathrow is now close to maximum handling capacity and very soon it will not be able to take any more flights. Planners now face a dilemma: how to provide more airport capacity in Southeast England. One alternative could be to build a new airport on reclaimed land in the Thames Estuary.

▶ Consolidating your thinking ◀

A planning proposal involving the location or route of a new piece of transport **infrastructure**, such as an airport or railway line, is almost always controversial with strong views 'for' and 'against'. A good example of this is the planned High Speed 2 (HS2) railway that will link London, Birmingham, Manchester and Leeds. This US$27 billion project will begin construction in 2017 and be operational by 2026.

Core High Speed network
Connecting High Speed line
'Classic compatible' routes
Potential future 'classic compatible' routes

Similarly, the three options for increasing air passenger and freight carrying capacity in Southeast England have very real costs and benefits depending on the perspective of different stakeholders. Geographers often refer to the two concepts of **accessibility** and **proximity** when considering the position of different stakeholders. Having accessibility to something (such as a new airport) refers to being able to reach and take advantage of what it offers without suffering any major disadvantages from it; whereas being in the close proximity of something like a new airport means that you are likely to experience more disadvantages than benefits from it. This is one reason why many people are in favour of constructing a new airport for London and Southeast England on reclaimed land in the Thames Estuary – maximising for the population the benefits of accessibility whilst minimising the disadvantages of proximity.

Research each of the following options and prepare a PowerPoint presentation to assist you in identifying and communicating to others the advantages and disadvantages of each proposal. Your presentation should also provide your considered view as to the best option for the way forward. This could, if you wish, include other considerations such as ideas on more sustainable forms of travel that might reduce the number of aircraft flights in the future and do away with the need to expand capacity.

Here are the schemes and some starting points for your research:

- Increase capacity at Heathrow by either building a new, third runway or lengthening one of the existing runways: http://www.bbc.co.uk/news/uk-19570653

- Build a second runway at Gatwick Airport: http://www.gatwickairport.com/business-community/New-runway/

- Construct a new hub airport on reclaimed land in the Thames Estuary. There are currently four competing schemes at different locations: http://www.airportwatch.org.uk/?page_id=307

▶▶

The economic arguments for building the railway are already being challenged by those who fear the potential impact on the environment and local communities along the route. See:

https://www.gov.uk/government/policies/developing-a-new-high-speed-rail-network/supporting-pages/reducing-the-impact-of-hs2-on-the-local-environment-and-communities

◀◀

2 Holes in the landscape

Why should we be concerned about sinkholes?

Read the full article on the BBC News website at:

http://www.bbc.co.uk/news/uk-26013121

'Car swallowed by 30ft sinkhole in Buckinghamshire'
BBC News, 3 February 2014

Imagine that you woke up one morning and looked out of your bedroom window to discover a 10 m deep hole in your driveway, into which your family car has disappeared. How would you feel? What would you do?

This is exactly what happened to Zoe Smith, who lives near High Wycombe in Buckinghamshire, one morning in February 2014. Her stepfather was alerted to the fact that something was wrong when he heard Zoe's screams and the words, 'My car, my car, it's gone!'

After feeling first shock and then relief that no-one was hurt, the family called the police and the fire brigade. They quickly discovered that Zoe's car had been swallowed by a **sinkhole**.

ATLANTIC

OCEAN

Europe

ICELAND

NORWAY

SWEDEN

FINLAND

ESTONIA

LATVIA

LITHUANIA

RUSSIA

UNITED
KINGDOM

DENMARK

IRELAND

NETHS.

GERMANY

POLAND

BELARUS

BELGIUM

CZECH
REP.

SLOVAKIA

UKRAINE

FRANCE

SWITZ.

AUSTRIA

HUNGARY

ROMANIA

PORTUGAL

SPAIN

ITALY

SERBIA

BULGARIA

GREECE

TURKEY

Outer Hebrides

Kirkwall

Thurso

Wick

Stornoway

Tarbert

Ullapool

Uig

Inverness

Ben
Macdui
▲
1309

Aberdeen

Fort William

Ben
Nevis
▲
1344

Grampian Mountains

Oban

Ben More
▲
1174

Perth

Dundee

Stirling

Glasgow

Edinburgh

Ayr

Southern Uplands

Berwick-upon-Tweed

North
Sea

Merrick
▲
843

Dumfries

Newcastle
upon Tyne

Coleraine

Antrim Hills

Larne

Carlisle

Sunderland

Londonderry
(Derry)

Belfast

Stranraer

Workington

Scafell
Pike
977 ▲

Darlington

Middlesbrough

Enniskillen

Scarborough

Newry

▲ 852
Slieve
Donard

KINGDOM

Pennines

York

Kingston upon Hull

Irish
Sea

Blackpool

Bradford

Leeds

Preston

Huddersfield

Grimsby

Holyhead

Liverpool

Manchester

Doncaster

Chester

Sheffield

Lincoln

Caernarfon

▲ 1085
Snowdon

Crewe

Stoke-on-
Trent

Nottingham

King's
Lynn

Derby

Cambrian Mountains

Shrewsbury

Wolverhampton

Peterborough

Norwich

Aberystwyth

Birmingham

Coventry

Cambridge

Ipswich

Northampton

Harwich

Fishguard

Hereford

Gloucester

Luton

Swansea

▲ 886

Newport

Oxford

Watford

Southend-on-Sea

Cardiff

Bristol

Swindon

London

Bath

Reading

Ashford

Dover

Salisbury

Brighton

Taunton

Southampton

Eastbourne

Exeter

▲
619

Weymouth

Bournemouth

Portsmouth

Plymouth

English Channel

FRANCE

St Neots

Cambridge

Bedford

Royston

Milton Keynes

East Anglian Heights

Sudbury

Leighton
Buzzard

Luton

Stevenage

Saffron
Walden

Braintree

Aylesbury

Chiltern Hills

Hertford

Harlow

Witham

Colchester

Oxford

Watford

Cheshunt

Chelmsford

High
Wycombe

London

Basildon

Southend-on-Sea

Reading

Staines

Greenwich

Gravesend

Sheerness

Bracknell

North Downs

Sittingbourne

Herne
Bay

Woking

Basingstoke

Guildford

Sevenoaks

Maidstone

Canterbury

Ashford

Crawley

Royal Tunbridge Wells

Horsham

Crowborough

South Downs

Hailsham

Hastings

Littlehampton

Brighton

Eastbourne

IRELAND

500 – 1000 m
200 – 500 m
0 – 200 m
Land below sea level

International boundary
Road
Railway
⊕ Airport
☐ Capital city

UNITED

On the other side of the world, in Guatemala City, a sinkhole that was 20 m wide and 30 m deep opened up in 2010. A three-storey factory and surrounding electricity poles were sucked into the hole, leaving fifteen people dead and several hundred at risk. This was not the first time that a sinkhole had devastated the city: in 2007, a 100 m deep sinkhole opened up, killing five people.

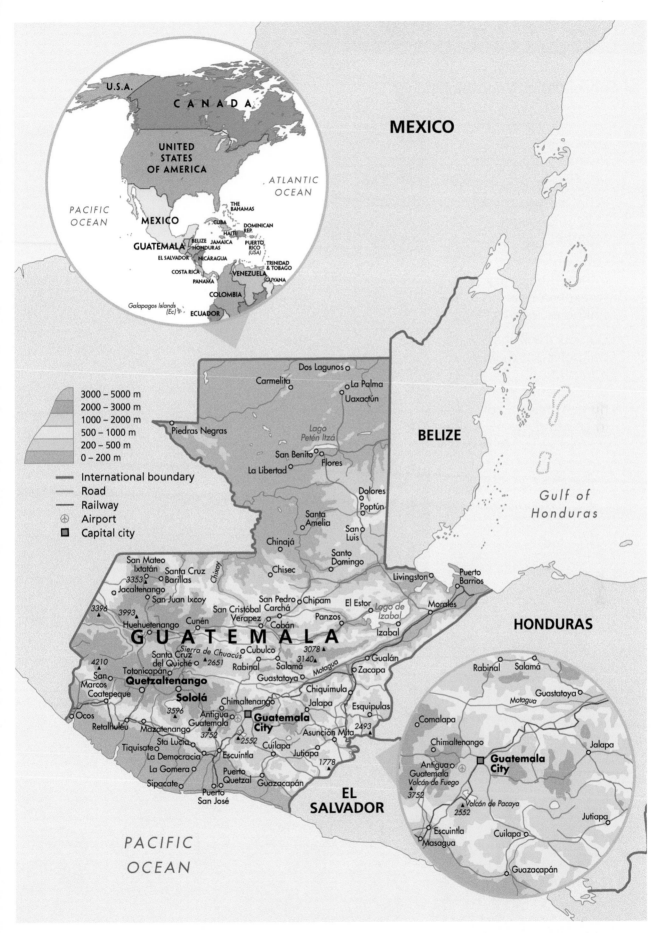

MEXICO

U.S.A.

C A N A D A

UNITED
STATES
OF AMERICA

*ATLANTIC
OCEAN*

*PACIFIC
OCEAN*

MEXICO

THE
BAHAMAS

CUBA

HAITI

DOMINICAN
REP.

GUATEMALA

BELIZE
HONDURAS

JAMAICA

PUERTO
RICO
(USA)

EL SALVADOR

NICARAGUA

COSTA RICA

PANAMA

VENEZUELA

TRINIDAD
& TOBAGO

GUYANA

COLOMBIA

*Galapagos Islands
(Ec)*

ECUADOR

3000 – 5000 m
2000 – 3000 m
1000 – 2000 m
500 – 1000 m
200 – 500 m
0 – 200 m

—— International boundary
—— Road
—— Railway
Airport
Capital city

Dos Lagunos

Carmelita

La Palma

Uaxactún

Piedras Negras

*Lago
Petén Itzá*

BELIZE

San Benito

Flores

La Libertad

Dolores

Poptún

Santa
Amelia

San
Luis

Chinajá

Santo
Domingo

Livingston

Puerto
Barrios

*Gulf of
Honduras*

San Mateo
Ixtatán

Santa Cruz
Barillas

Chixoy

Chisec

3353

Jacaltenango

San Juan Ixcoy

San Pedro
Carchá

Chipam

El Estor

*Lago de
Izabal*

Morales

3398

3993

San Cristóbal
Verapez

Cobán

Panzos

Izabal

HONDURAS

Huehuetenango

Cunén

G U A T E M A L A

Cubulco

3078

Gualán

Sierra de Chuacús

Santa Cruz
del Quiché

2651

3140

Motagua

Zacapa

4210

Rabinal

Salamá

San
Marcos

Totonicapán

Guastatoya

Chiquimula

Rabinal

Salamá

Coatepeque

Quetzaltenango

Sololá

Chimaltenango

Jalapa

Esquipulas

Guastatoya

Motagua

3596

Antigua
Guatemala

**Guatemala
City**

2493

Comalapa

Ocos

Retalhuleu

Mazatenango

3752

Asunción Mita

Chimaltenango

Jalapa

Tiquisate

Sta Lucía

2552

Cuilapa

Jutiapa

Antigua
Guatemala

**Guatemala
City**

La Democracia

Escuintla

1778

Volcán de Fuego

La Gomera

3752

Sipacate

Puerto
Quetzal

Guazacapán

**EL
SALVADOR**

Volcán de Pacaya

2552

Jutiapa

Puerto
San José

Escuintla

Cuilapa

Masagua

*PACIFIC

OCEAN*

Guazacapán

► Consolidating your thinking ◄

- Look at the images and map on pp. 30–31.
- What do you think links the images together?
- Can you use the information to try to explain how sinkholes form?
- Do you think that sinkholes are mainly a natural phenomenon or do humans have a role in creating them? ►►

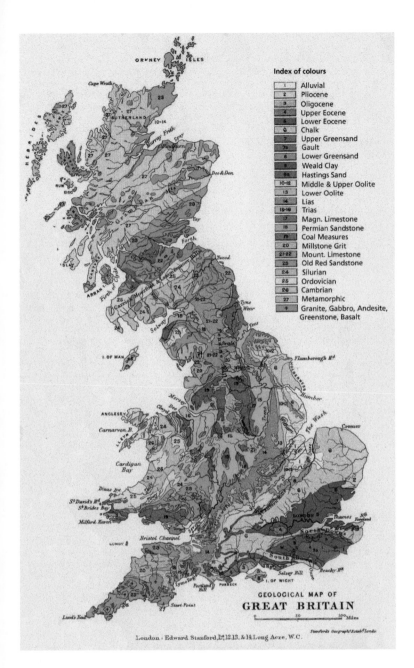

Index of colours

1	Alluvial
2	Pliocene
3	Oligocene
4	Upper Eocene
5	Lower Eocene
6	Chalk
7	Upper Greensand
7a	Gault
8	Lower Greensand
9	Weald Clay
9a	Hastings Sand
10-12	Middle & Upper Oolite
13	Lower Oolite
14	Lias
15-16	Trias
17	Magn. Limestone
18	Permian Sandstone
19	Coal Measures
20	Millstone Grit
21-22	Mount. Limestone
23	Old Red Sandstone
24	Silurian
25	Ordovician
26	Cambrian
27	Metamorphic
4	Granite, Gabbro, Andesite, Greenstone, Basalt

GEOLOGICAL MAP OF
GREAT BRITAIN

London : Edward Stanford, Lᵈ 12,13, & 14 Long Acre, W.C.

▶ Consolidating your thinking ◀

• Using the map on page 27 to help you, locate the following five UK cities: London, Manchester, Bristol, Cardiff, Glasgow.

• According to the **geology** map above, what type of rock lies beneath each of these cities?

• Pick one of the cities, research the type of rock it lies on and create a factsheet about it. Is it an **igneous**, **metamorphic** or **sedimentary** rock? What are its characteristics and properties? Include an image to show what the rock looks like.

• Do you think sinkholes are likely to occur in the city you have chosen? Why do you think this?

Watch a video of this process at:

http://www.bbc.co.uk/news/science-environment-25983415

The weathering process described on this page is called **solution**. Use the activity in the Teacher Book (p.18) to create a storyboard of this process. Make sure that your captions for each of the images are clear and thorough.

The key to explaining how sinkholes form is to look underground at the area's geology. Sinkholes are more likely to form in areas where the rock dissolves when it comes into contact with rainwater; for example, **limestone** or **chalk**. Rainwater is already naturally acidic as water combines with carbon dioxide in the atmosphere and also absorbs more CO_2 as it seeps into the ground and reacts with decaying vegetables.

The acidic rainfall reacts with and dissolves the underlying rock, creating large **caverns**. When the soil above is no longer supported, it collapses into the cavern to create a sinkhole, a process that can take anything from a couple of minutes to several hours.

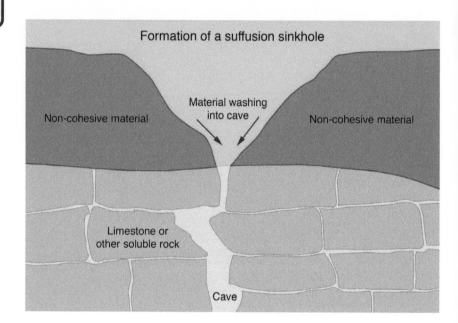

Formation of a suffusion sinkhole

Non-cohesive material

Material washing into cave

Non-cohesive material

Limestone or other soluble rock

Cave

However, human processes can also lead to the creation of sinkholes. For example, the sinkhole in Guatemala City was probably caused by water pipes below the city breaking and overflowing. Guatemala City has volcanic ash as its main rock type and so it is likely that the extra water in the pipes washed these deposits away instead of dissolving them. Abandoned mines, where people have previously industrially extracted the rock, can also occasionally cause sinkholes to occur.

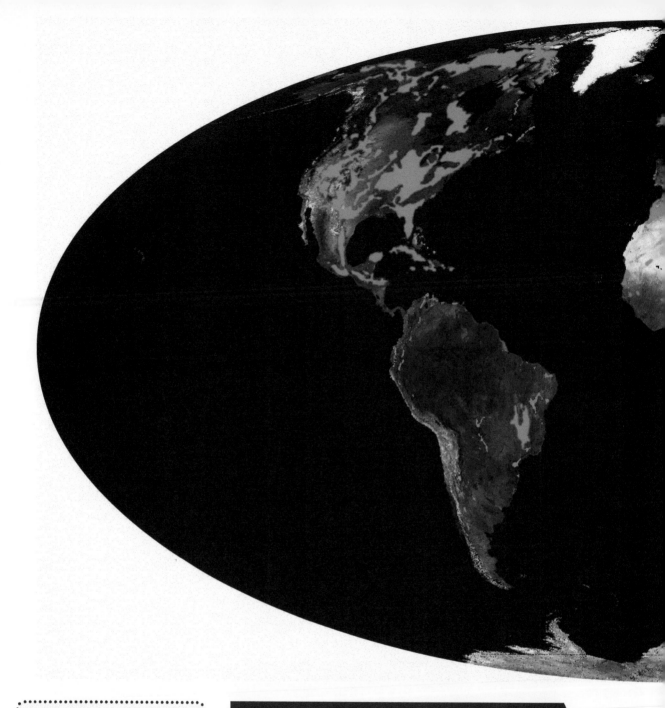

- Look at the map showing the pattern of carbonate outcrops.
- Using an atlas, can you describe the pattern?
- Do you think that this is a useful map to use to predict where sinkholes are likely to occur?

2.2 Where are sinkholes likely to occur?

▶ Consolidating your thinking ◀

From the map it is clear that much of the USA (approximately 40%) has **carbonate outcrops** (mainly limestone and chalk), which make up its underlying geology. However, these rocks are not spread evenly so there are some states that have a higher incidence of sinkholes than others. For example, the state of Missouri has limestone and **dolomite** (a sedimentary, carbonate rock) underneath it, whilst the geology of the state of Florida is mainly limestone.

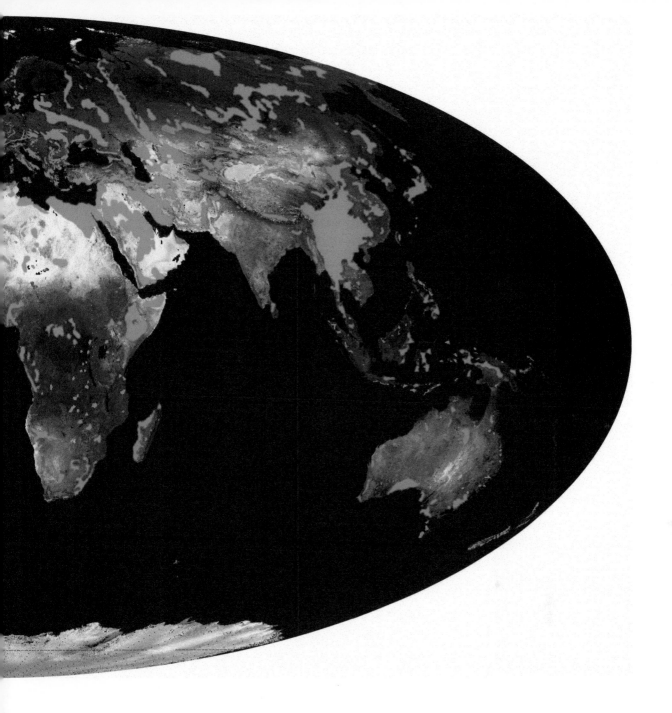

This begins to explain why these states tend to have higher incidence than others, with Florida being termed the 'sinkhole capital' of the USA. However, this isn't the whole story, as the climate and the way that Florida's land is used also have significant roles.

Florida has a **humid climate** with over 1500 mm of rainfall annually and temperatures of between 20 °C and 30 °C throughout the year. Have a go at the activity in the Teacher Book that looks at the climate of Florida in more detail. This seasonal rainfall, which is usually caused by **hurricanes** in the summer months, means that vast amounts of rain can fall in a short space of time. This adds weight to the soil and causes the roofs of caves to collapse. In the dry season (from November to April), where **drought** conditions prevail, the **water table** can lower by so much that the pressure in the underground caverns is reduced and the sides can collapse.

> Complete the learning activity about the climate in Miami, Florida on p.19 of the Teacher Book.

The way that the people of Florida use the land also makes sinkholes more likely. The soil is very fertile and this, combined with the warm, wet climate, makes the area perfect for agriculture. Citrus trees and soft fruits are a particular speciality and are irrigated using **groundwater** from Florida's underground **aquifers**. The pumping of the water can cause the water table to drop by tens of metres in a very short space of time. When this has happened in the past, sinkholes have opened up in large numbers around the drained aquifer.

2.3 What problems do sinkholes create?

People living in Florida are clearly quite worried about sinkholes and the potential effect this could have on their lives and property. The number of home **insurance** claims in Florida has risen dramatically in recent years, increasing from 2360 in 2006 to about 6500 in 2013.

Part of the reason for this is that builders are having to go further out of the cities and develop more sinkhole-prone sites in order to satisfy the state's demand for housing. It is also the case that sinkholes, unlike hurricanes which also wreak havoc on Florida, are unpredictable and there is little in the way of technology to solve the problem. As a result, all homes in the 'Swiss cheese state' are required to have some form of insurance against 'catastrophic ground collapse', which usually costs between US$200 and US$2000 per year, depending on the home's location and associated risk. In addition to this, for most insurance premiums the excess for sinkholes (the amount you have to pay if you make a claim) begins at US$25,000.

It is not just homes that are at risk. Florida, and particularly the city of Orlando, is famous for its theme parks, including Epcot, Disney's Magic Kingdom, Universal Studios and Legoland, which attract fifty-one million tourists and contribute US$51 billion to Florida's economy each year. In August 2013, a sinkhole opened up less than five miles from Walt Disney World. More recently, on 29 May 2014, a sinkhole opened up in the car park opposite Legoland. At 8.30 a.m., the depression was estimated to be 30 ft wide and 5 ft deep but by 6 p.m. that evening, it had expanded to 85 ft wide and 18 ft deep. Fortunately, because it was discovered before Legoland had opened, there were no casualties and no cars were damaged.

Sadly, sinkholes can cause fatalities, although there has only been one in Florida in recent decades. In February 2013, 37-year-old Jeff Bush was killed by a sinkhole. His home in Seffner, a suburb of Tampa, disappeared into the 100 ft deep hole whilst he slept, although five other people in the house managed to escape unharmed. Jeff's brother, Jeremy, heard his brother's screams and tried to pull him out, without success. The next day, authorities called off the search for Jeff as they could detect no signs of life.

Understandably, the tragedy caused shockwaves throughout Florida and the USA as a whole. The house has now been demolished and the family hope that they can create a memorial at the site. Clearly, in Florida and other parts of the world which are underlain by carbonate rocks or in areas where water pipes are poorly maintained, sinkholes can be a huge problem for the people living there. However, sinkholes can also be massive tourist attractions and can provide great benefits.

AREA 1. Bare or thinly covered limestone
Sinkholes are few, generally shallow and broad and develop gradually. Solution sinkholes dominate.

AREA 2. Cover is 30 to 200 feet thick
Consists mainly of incohesive and permeable sand. Sinkholes are few, shallow, of small diameter, and develop gradually. Cover-subsidence sinkholes dominate.

AREA 3. Cover is 30 to 200 feet thick
Consists mainly of cohesive clayey sediments of low permeabiity. Sinkholes are most numerous, of varying size,and develop abruptly. Cover-collapse sinkholes dominate.

AREA 4. Cover is more than 200 feet thick
Consists of cohesive sediments interlayed with discontinuous carbonate beds. Sinkholes are very few, but several large diameter, deep sinkholes occur. Cover-collapse sinkholes dominate.

You can read more about the features of Belize's eco-tourism here:

http://www.belize.com/eco

Complete the activity in the Teacher Book (pp.20–21) which investigates the importance of Belize's tourist industry in more detail.

2.4 Are sinkholes really a problem?

Divers off the coast of Belize can swim in the Great Blue Hole: a flooded sinkhole where species of fish, including the midnight parrot fish and the Caribbean reef shark, can be found. These natural attractions have led to the development of a thriving tourism industry, particularly in Belize; in 2012, nearly one million tourists visited and tourism generated around 20% of the country's **gross domestic product (GDP)**.

The Prime Minister of Belize has declared that he will use tourism to combat poverty, and the growth of tourism has had positive knock-on effects in agriculture, commerce and the construction industry. At the same time, eco-tourism is growing significantly in Belize with many hotels focusing on energy efficiency and using renewable resources.

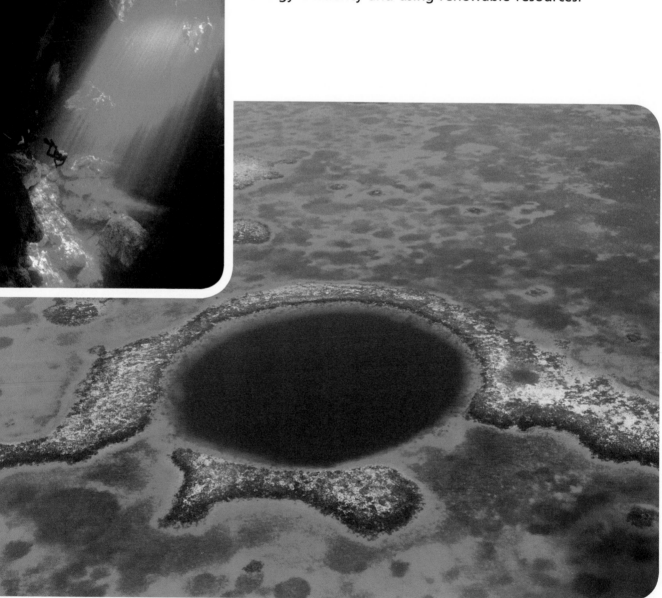

▶ Consolidating your thinking ◀

Shoe-box sinkholes

You are going to create an *annotated model* to bring all of this information together and to help you answer the key question at the beginning of the enquiry. Use the information on the previous pages, plus additional reading of your own (additional sources are recommended below) to *demonstrate that you understand* the geographical reasons that explain why we should be concerned about sinkholes.

STEP 1

Take a small box (a shoe-box is an ideal size) and cut a hole about 5 cm in diameter into the lid. This will represent the sinkhole.

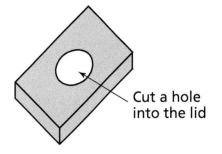

Cut a hole into the lid

STEP 2

Decorate the outside of the lid of the box to show the *characteristics* of the location of your sinkhole. Is it in the suburbs of Guatemala City, the farms of Florida, off the coast of Belize or somewhere else?

You could use cardboard, sand, modelling clay, etc. to make the landscape as realistic as possible. Have a look at the following website to see some other ideas for landscapes in a box:

http://www.geographypods.com/landscape-in-a-box.html

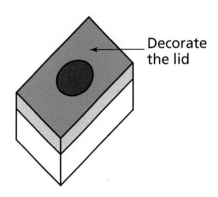

Decorate the lid

STEP 3

On the inside of the lid, stick a map to show the *location* of your sinkhole. Think about what scale map or maps will show the location most effectively – you may need one or two maps. Also on the inside of the lid, next to your map, stick a short paragraph that describes the location of your sinkhole.

Remember to use geographical vocabulary in your description. Names of continents, countries and places, and points of the compass are all useful features to include. Draw arrows from your paragraph to the relevant places on your map so that it becomes *annotated*.

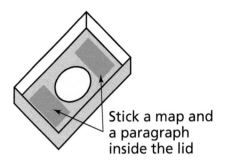

Stick a map and a paragraph inside the lid

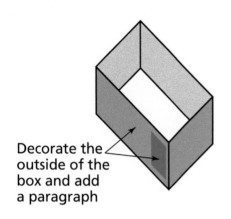

Decorate the outside of the box and add a paragraph

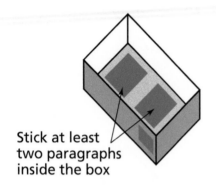

Stick at least two paragraphs inside the box

Additional sources of information to extend the depth and breadth of your explanation:

Useful general websites about sinkholes:

http://www.bbc.co.uk/news/science-environment-26242258

http://www.independent.co.uk/news/science/sinkholes-what-are-they-how-do-they-form-and-why-are-we-seeing-so-many-9136235.html

http://www.theguardian.com/world/sinkholes

http://www.newscientist.com/article/dn23256-briefing-the-strange-science-of-sinkholes.html#.UyWvXoWBfiE

STEP 4

Decorate the outside of the box to show what is happening below the ground to cause the sinkhole to form. You can stick a paragraph describing and explaining why your sinkhole has formed on the outside of your box.

Make sure you consider and answer the following questions: What is the geology like? What physical processes have resulted in the formation of your sinkhole? Are there any human processes that have contributed to its formation? Again, try to make sure that you draw arrows to link your images and decoration to the explanation to create annotations.

STEP 5

On the inside of your box you need to stick at least two paragraphs. The first should describe *the effects of sinkholes*. A resource to help you think about the effects and ways of classifying them is available to print off from the Teacher Book (pp.22–23).

You also need a *concluding paragraph*, which is a summary of the main points and *answers the question*. Look to apply appropriate connectives such as 'in conclusion', 'in summary', 'to sum up', 'overall', 'on the whole', 'in short', 'in brief', 'to conclude', 'so to round off', etc.

An example of some of the annotations a pupil has written for their model is available in the Teacher Book (p.24). What do you like about their annotations? What could be improved? Have they made their annotations clear so that you understand how their sinkhole was formed? Does the conclusion answer the question: *'Why should we be concerned about sinkholes?'*

Have a look at one of your partner's draft paragraphs. Highlight any geographical vocabulary that they use. Do they explain what these terms mean? In a different colour, highlight any places where they don't use geographical vocabulary but could do so. What vocabulary would you recommend?

2.5 Are sinkholes becoming more common?

Whilst underlying geology is unlikely to change much in the short term, climate, and particularly the amounts and patterns of rainfall, *is* likely to alter as a result of increased amounts of **greenhouse gases** (such as CO_2) in our atmosphere. Quite what is going to happen to rainfall is difficult to predict; some areas might have more rainfall, others may have less, although in general the global average is expected to increase and storm events are likely to be more intense. Should this happen, the incidence of sinkhole formation is likely to increase.

- Look carefully at the map that shows the estimated change in precipitation rates by the end of the twenty-first century (be careful, the figures are in inches not millimetres).

- Which locations are likely to see more precipitation?

- Which locations are likely to see less?

Estimated change in precipitation by the end of the twenty-first century

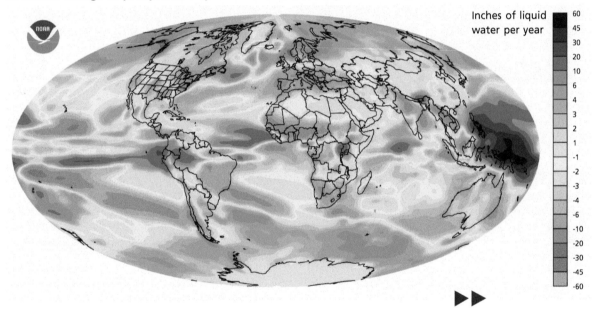

Inches of liquid water per year

	60
	45
	30
	20
	10
	6
	4
	3
	2
	1
	-1
	-2
	-3
	-4
	-6
	-10
	-20
	-30
	-45
	-60

▶▶

http://www.theguardian.com/environment/2014/feb/21/sinkholes-uk-wet-winter

http://www.independent.co.uk/environment/more-sinkholes-will-open-up-across-britain-as-the-effects-of-flooding-continue-warns-british-geological-survey-9139276.html

http://www.telegraph.co.uk/topics/weather/10643787/More-sinkholes-expected-to-swallow-up-Britain.html

▶ Consolidating your thinking ◀

Read the articles on the websites listed in the side panel. The articles suggest that 2013/2014, the wettest winter on record, was also a record year for sinkhole formation in the UK.

Why are sinkholes more likely to occur after intense storm events? Do you think that the UK should be prepared for more sinkholes to occur in the future? Justify your thinking. You could use the sheet in the Teacher Book (p.25) to support and extend your answer.

3 Is fracking all that it's cracked up to be?

Is fracking a sustainable solution to the UK's energy security challenge?

3.1 Why is the population of Williston, North Dakota increasing so fast?

The images on the next page show a farm outside of Williston in North Dakota in the USA, which was a sleepy agricultural town with a population of 12,512 in the year 2000. By 2013 its population had reached an estimated 20,085. The mayor believes it is even higher, with an estimated 30,000 people calling Williston home.

This area of North Dakota has a semi-arid climate, with freezing temperatures possible from late September to mid May each year. Prior to 2006, the majority of jobs in the area were on farms or in local shops. Today, this area has the lowest unemployment rate in the USA and the Walmart store pays wages that are double its national average.

However, soaring rent costs mean some people have to sleep in their cars and the area has experienced an increase in social problems like drug dealing, domestic violence and other crimes. The **infrastructure** and **services** here have struggled to grow at a quick enough pace to support the rise in population.

There are four years between the two aerial images on the next page. What changes can you describe?

▶▶

Figure A: *Farmland outside of Williston, North Dakota in 2009*

Figure B: *Farmland outside of Williston, North Dakota in 2014*

► Consolidating your thinking ◄

Examine the range of photographs and graphs in Figures A–G. These should allow you to build up a story that helps in answering Question 3.1. Spend some time examining the photographs and graphs and form an explanation. Share your ideas with a partner in discussion and put together a **photo story** that answers Question 3.1. You might want to do some extra research to help with your thinking.

The Bakken Shale Formation, an extensive source rock for oil and one of the largest locations of fracking in the United States.

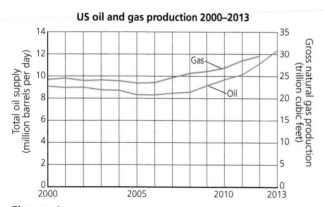

Figure A

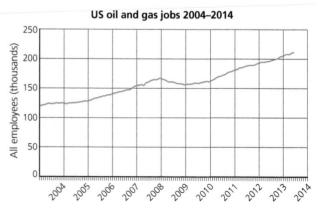

Figure B

Figure C

Figure D

Figure E

Figure F

Williston,
North Dakota

Figure G:
*Gas flares in
North
Dakota are
visible from
space*

Each different energy source has advantages and disadvantages to people, **economies** and the environment when it is used. The information table in the Teacher Book (pp.28–29) outlines some of these for each type of energy source shown on the energy landscape in Figure A. We can classify all of the energy sources into two groups:

- **Renewable energy** sources can be used again and again.

- **Non-renewable energy** sources will eventually run out.

▶▶

3.2 Are our energy sources renewable or non-renewable?

The oil boom that has driven the population growth in Williston is part of a wider dramatic increase in the oil and gas production of the USA. Shale rocks are being explored by geologists and new techniques for extraction have been developed. This, alongside the recovery of oil from **tar sands** in Canada, has significantly changed where the USA is sourcing its increasing **energy** supplies from. However, these unconventional sources are finite and once they have been extracted and consumed they are gone for good.

From powering our laptops and smart phones, to heating our houses and boiling our water, we are all using an increasing amount of energy each year. Global population increase and rising levels of economic development mean that this pattern is repeated across the world.

Humans use a wide range of sources to provide us with energy for heating, power and transportation. Much of our power is generated by using energy sources to create heat. This heat is used to turn water into steam, which turns giant turbines that make electricity. This is known as thermal power generation. Currently, the UK generates the

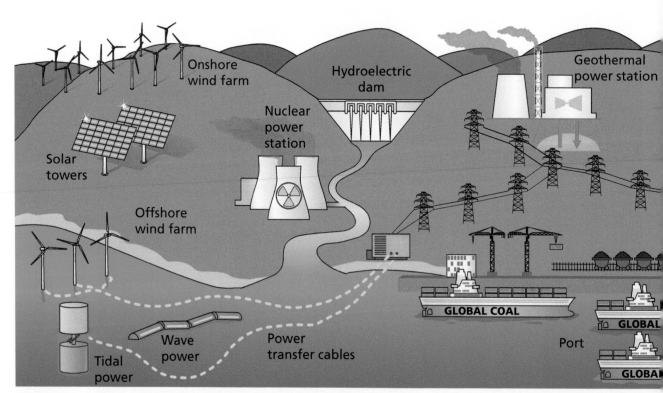

Figure A

vast majority of its electricity in thermal power stations. The sources of energy available to each country vary around the world. Countries with plentiful supplies and the technology to use them are described as *energy secure*.

Try to manage your own energy landscape by playing *Electrocity* at:

http://www.electrocity. co.nz/

▶ Consolidating your thinking ◀

Using the resources in this enquiry, as well as the information table from the Teacher Book (pp.28–29), you will need to categorise each of the energy sources into renewable or non-renewable energy resources.

You could also try to think about any other ways of classifying these such as 'environmental impact' or 'most to least important, today and in 2030'. You should also use the information from the Teacher Book to put together your own energy landscape like the one on this page, with researched images of each different source.

Your work should develop the advantages and disadvantages of each source in the table and will ideally show the different methods of classifying the energy source. For example, coal would be classified as non-renewable and as a **fossil fuel**. You could present the outcomes of your work as a poster, a model or a sketch map.

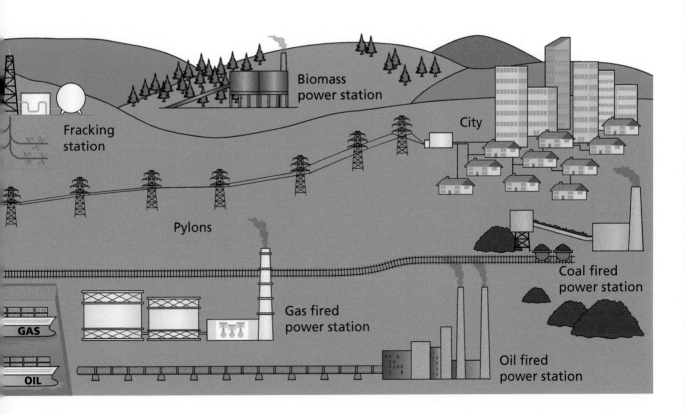

You should now be secure in your understanding of how to classify energy sources into renewable or non-renewable energy resources. Each country in the world will use a range of different energy sources to produce electricity, using some renewables like wind power, but mostly non-renewables like oil, coal and gas. However, there are some exceptions, such as Germany, which already fulfils 74% of its power needs using renewable sources. The range of sources used is described as the **energy mix** of a country.

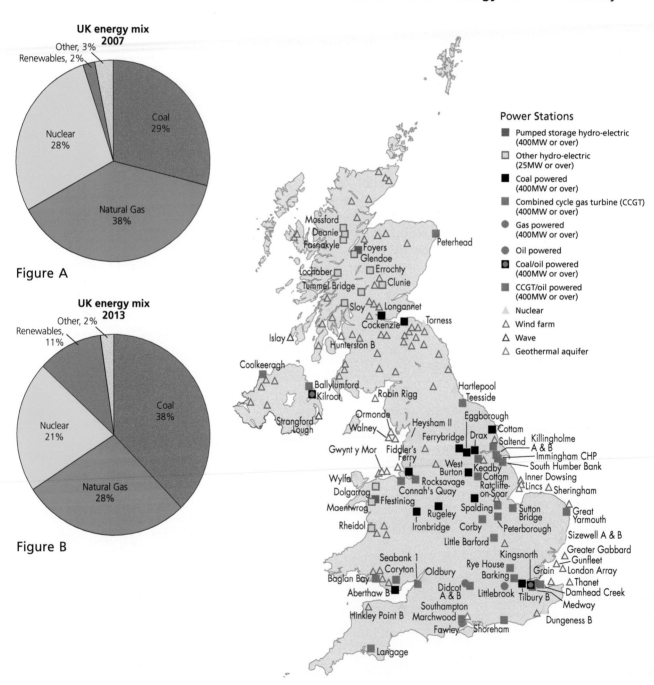

UK energy mix 2007

Other, 3%
Renewables, 2%
Coal 29%
Nuclear 28%
Natural Gas 38%

Figure A

UK energy mix 2013

Other, 2%
Renewables, 11%
Coal 38%
Nuclear 21%
Natural Gas 28%

Figure B

Power Stations

- ■ Pumped storage hydro-electric (400MW or over)
- □ Other hydro-electric (25MW or over)
- ■ Coal powered (400MW or over)
- ■ Combined cycle gas turbine (CCGT) (400MW or over)
- ● Gas powered (400MW or over)
- ● Oil powered (400MW or over)
- ⬡ Coal/oil powered (400MW or over)
- ■ CCGT/oil powered (400MW or over)
- ▲ Nuclear
- △ Wind farm
- △ Wave
- △ Geothermal aquifer

In the UK and in many other countries, the energy mix has changed significantly over time. As sources of energy are discovered, exploited and exhausted, the way a country generates its electricity will also need to change. For example, the UK had plentiful supplies of accessible coal, so this was used in the earliest power stations. The invention of nuclear power stations, combined with the availability of cheaper coal from countries such as Poland and government disputes with miners, saw the beginning of mines being closed in the 1970s. This led to a decline in the use of coal, which accelerated with the discovery of reserves of oil and natural gas in the North Sea and resulted in the closure of most of the UK's coal mines in the 1980s.

Figures A and B (opposite) show how the UK energy mix has shifted since 2007, when natural gas and nuclear power accounted for over 50% of electricity produced. By 2013, this had shifted again as renewables have begun to increase in importance and the UK has taken advantage of importing low-priced coal from abroad. However, the UK is clearly still predominantly reliant on non-renewable fossil fuels for electricity generation. In 2013 the country became a net importer of these for the first time because reserves in the North Sea are in decline. The UK also needs to phase out older nuclear power stations, as well as those older coal- and gas-fired power stations that emit the most carbon dioxide into the atmosphere.

▶ Consolidating your thinking ◀

A country that is heavily reliant on the import of energy sources, or one that is reliant on non-renewable sources, could be described as energy insecure because they do not control access to these resources and are vulnerable to sudden interruptions in supply or price increases. The UK faces many challenges because of its current energy mix and the implications of this for security and keeping the lights on.

- Examine the map of UK electricity-generating power stations, Figures A and B (the pie-charts of UK energy mix over time) and the data tables that show the key countries the UK uses as sources of imported energy.

- Your challenge is to produce an *infographic* around the theme 'UK energy security'.

- You might want to consider using a website like http://www.piktochart.com/, http://www.easel.ly/ or http://www.infogr.am/ to help you.

- Try to include maps, graphs and images. You could cover past and current patterns, the distribution of power stations, the pathways that the UK energy imports take and how sustainable you consider the current position is.

- How reliable do you think the UK's energy imports are?

UK coal imports – largest sources % 2012
Russia 40%
Columbia 26%
USA 24%

UK crude oil – largest sources % 2012
Norway 50%
Nigeria 12%
Russia 11%
Algeria 6%

UK gas imports – largest sources % 2012
Norway 55%
Netherlands 15%
Qatar 27%

3.4 Is fracking a sustainable solution to the UK's energy security challenge?

The USA is currently experiencing a domestic energy boom with the discovery and exploitation of unconventional oil and gas sources like those found in North Dakota. This has drastically reduced its reliance on foreign energy imports and increased the short-term energy security of the world's largest consumer of energy.

However, the USA is still reliant on non-renewable fossil fuels for 67% of its energy needs, which significantly adds to global **carbon emissions**.

In Question 3.3 you examined the UK energy mix and the energy security challenges faced by the government in keeping the lights on in the future. One possible solution to the UK's energy needs is to explore and exploit the huge potential reserves of natural gas locked up in shale rocks found beneath some areas of the country.

Supporters of this move point to the USA and suggest the UK could also experience a vital domestic energy boom by exploiting its gas reserves in shale rocks. However, this is not without huge controversy and there is significant local opposition to the drilling, with many groups arguing that this is not a sustainable solution.

▶ Consolidating your thinking ◀

Now you are going to plan and carry out your own geographical enquiry, which should reach an informed conclusion about how you feel about the fracking debate.

You can conduct research into this issue, using the resources on the following pages as a starting point. Your aim is to produce your own enquiry into fracking in the UK.

There are several key stages in planning and carrying out a geographical enquiry, as Figure A on the following page shows.

- How can the UK meet its energy needs, maintain security of supplies and meet its global commitment to reducing carbon emissions?
- Is fracking for shale gas a sustainable solution?

▶▶

Your enquiry could be presented in a variety of ways, such as a presentation, a leaflet or a poster. Discuss your ideas with your teacher.

▶▶

How do I go about a geographical enquiry?

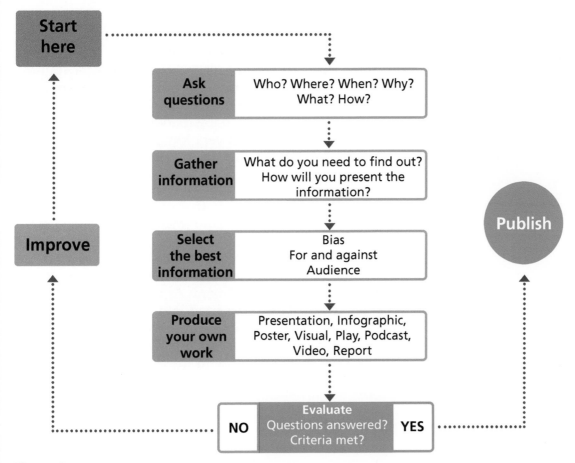

Figure A

Start by mind mapping as many questions as possible around the central issue 'Fracking in the UK' and then:

• Consider questions about the natural environment, the economy, people and decision-making.

• Select your strongest five or six questions and put these in a logical sequence.

• Follow the remaining steps in the enquiry sequence diagram.

Remember, your fracking enquiry must reach a conclusion to the question '*Is fracking a sustainable solution to the UK's energy security?*' Sustainability refers to meeting the needs of people today, without degrading the environment or affecting the ability of future generations to meet their own needs locally and globally. It is important therefore that your work makes an informed judgement on what role, if any, shale gas from fracking has to play in the UK energy mix.

Factfile 1: Shale and fracking basics

Shale is a dull-looking, dark grey or black, soft, sedimentary rock that is incredibly common. 70% of the world's surface rocks are sedimentary and 50% of these are shale. Shale contains 95% of all the organic matter found in sedimentary rocks. It is found at a depth of 2–3 km in parts of the UK. Under the microscope it is very fine-grained and there are tiny spaces between each of the grains. Shale rocks also have very low **permeability**, which means that liquids and gases do not pass through easily.

Shale is formed from **sediments** that contained large amounts of organic matter (plant remains). 330 million years ago, in the **Carboniferous** period, rivers carrying large quantities of organic matter flowed into shallow seas and deposited this material. Over time, the material was buried under layer after layer of sediment. As the organic matter was buried, it was slowly converted into methane by bacteria or, more commonly, by heating. This methane, or shale gas, is the same as is burned in your home or in power stations. It is 'glued' into the shale rocks due to the tiny spaces between the particles. This makes it extremely hard to extract, so it is referred to as unconventional gas. In some places, the shale rocks contain gas and oil together – this is dependent on the geological conditions in which they were formed.

A sample of shale rock

To get at the gas and oil locked in the impermeable rocks, the rocks have to be fractured by pumping chemical hydraulic fluid at very high pressure into wells. These fluids crack the rock and create fractures in the target rock formation. The process of hydraulic fracturing or 'fracking', allows the gas or oil to flow up the well as the fractures are propped open by the fracture fluid.

The stages of exploration, drilling and production

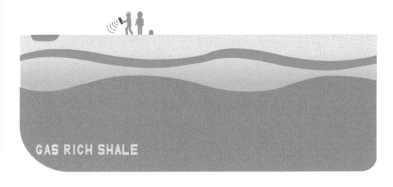

1. First, **geophysicists** fire **seismic waves** into the ground to survey the area and build maps of the underlying geology.

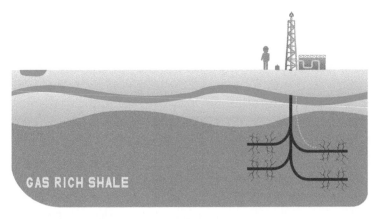

2. If planning permission is granted, exploration wells are drilled and samples taken. The well is flow tested and some fracturing might take place. Any gas will be burned. A decision on whether enough gas is present to make the well cost-effective is taken.

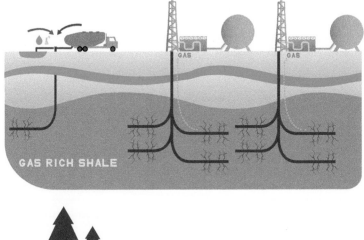

3. If the well site is suitable then more wells will be drilled in a cluster. Water, chemicals and equipment will have to be transported to the site. Waste fracking fluid will have to be stored and gas pipelines may have to be built.

4. Eventually, the gas will be exhausted and the site should be returned to its original condition.

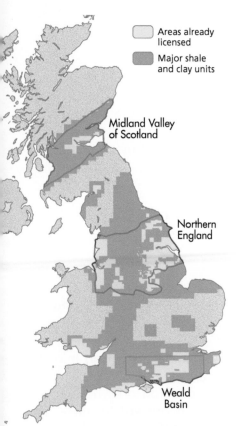

Figure A: *Map of the UK showing areas that contain shale rocks and basins that might contain gas or oil*

Factfile 2: What is the potential for shale gas in the UK?

There are a number of areas of the UK with estimated shale gas or oil resources. The British Geological Survey (BGS) has been studying these areas and producing resource estimates. The two key areas are the Bowland formation found mainly in Lancashire and the Weald basin in the southeast (mainly Sussex and Surrey). Recent BGS reports have suggested:

- The Bowland formation *could* contain 37.6 trillion cubic metres of gas.

- The Weald basin is unlikely to contain any gas, but *could* contain 4.4 billion barrels of oil.

These resource figures estimate the entire volume of gas and oil contained in the rock formation, not how much can be recovered. It is thought that only a fraction of the resource could be recovered and substantial further investigation through drilling is required. One scientist has suggested that the Bowland formation could require 33,000 wells.

A number of companies have licences to drill but only a few have actually begun the process. In May 2014, the UK government announced a new law that allows companies to drill underneath private land in a bid to free up companies from laws that restrict operations. It is clear that the industry is in its infancy in the UK.

Advantages	Disadvantages
These resources could improve the future energy security of the UK by reducing the need for imports.	Shale oil and gas are still finite, non-renewable fossil fuels that release CO_2 into the atmosphere. They will not help meet targets for carbon emission reduction.
Gas is seen as 'greener' than coal as it produces less CO_2, so supporters argue that fracking helps reduce CO_2 emissions.	There are concerns over the chemical waste water and contamination of water supplies by the fracking fluid and gas.
Fracking could provide thousands of new energy jobs in the UK.	Sites will see an increase in traffic that will disrupt communities.
These resources could also reduce the energy bills for households. The USA saw a 70% decrease in gas prices.	There is concern that money for fracking will take money away from investment into renewable energy.
The companies have proposed community benefits such as payments when the well is started and 1% of the money it makes.	Fracking has caused minor localised earthquakes. This has caused the UK government to stop drilling while investigations take place.
As technology develops, more oil and gas could be recovered in the future.	There are concerns about methane leaking from the drilling sites.

3.5 Are there alternatives?

Supporters of fracking point to the need to reduce energy imports and to meet the UK's demand from domestic supplies. They see fracking as a potentially cheap option. However, it is likely to take years to come on stream and critics say the environmental risks of drilling are too high, in addition to the need to radically reduce carbon emissions to avoid more extreme climate change. There will continue to be heated debate regarding this issue in the coming years.

► Consolidating your thinking ◄

There are alternatives to fracking, each with its own disadvantages and benefits, that could help improve the UK's energy security.

You will need to consider some of these alternative options before devising an energy plan for an area of the UK. You will need to make geographical decisions based on the information provided, your own knowledge and the understanding you have developed so far throughout this enquiry.

- Use the images on pages 56 and 57 and the factfiles from the Teacher Book (pp.30–32) to examine the costs and benefits of each of these alternative energy sources. You could create an A3 mind map with the information or use an online collaborative tool like *MindMeister* to work with a partner.

- Using the energy proposals, map, and information table from the Teacher Book (pp.33–35), you will be making decisions about the energy future of an area of Devon in the United Kingdom. Carefully consider the guidance given to make informed and justified geographical decisions.

As you have seen throughout this enquiry, meeting the energy needs of people today and in the future is complex and there are no easy decisions. Geographers all around the world have to advise governments and energy companies on the costs and benefits of different energy solutions as countries try to shift their energy mix away from finite fossil fuels and towards more sustainable solutions.

However, many of the alternatives are not without controversy. In this final extension task you will need to once again examine each of the images on these pages.

For each image you will need to:

• Ensure you can name and categorise each type of energy source.

• Name and locate on a world map specific places where this energy source has been exploited successfully. How viable are these energy sources in your country?

You will need to select one of the following issues surrounding these alternatives to fracking and use it as a basis for research:

- Does nuclear power have a long term future after the Fukushima nuclear disaster in Japan?

- Should the River Severn Tidal Barrage in the UK be built?

- Do wind farms enhance or damage the natural environment?

- Can renewable energy ever really meet our increasing energy demands?

- Should we be changing our energy sources or our behaviour?

You should carefully research one of the questions and develop an opinion backed up by justified reasons. You will need to present your research and opinions in the form of a two minute video or speech to your class. Ensure that you draw on all the skills, knowledge and understanding that you have developed throughout this enquiry.

4 Almost Armageddon!

Why did the earth nearly die at the end of the Permian period?

The story of the earth from its formation around 4.6 billion years ago to the present is divided into **geological** time periods. Each geological period reveals tantalising glimpses into our past. For geographers the most fascinating and frightening glimpse of all is perhaps what we see at the end of the **Permian** period, 252 million years ago – a time when 96% of all living things were wiped from the face of the earth and our planet came very, very close to dying. This enquiry is about finding out what happened to cause the Great Dying back then, why it matters to know and why we all need to be very grateful for the survival instincts of a certain creature called *Thrinaxodon*.

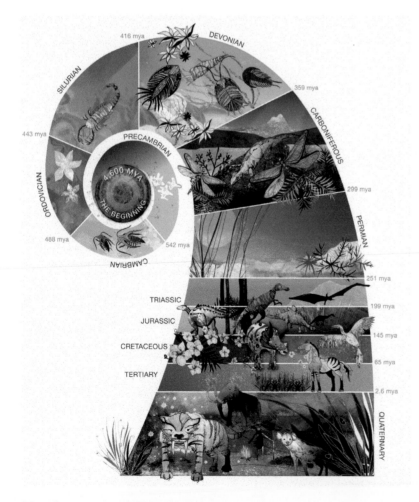

Skara Brae Neolithic settlement in Orkney (3000 BC, but only 0.0006 mm back along the 100 m timeline)

Stonehenge (3100 BC and the world's most famous stone circle, but only 0.0006 mm back along the 100 m timeline)

4.1 What is 'deep time' and where can I find it?

Outside in the playground or on the playing field, measure 100 m with a tape or pace 100 steps as evenly as possible. Mark the beginning and the end of the line with pegs. The peg furthest away represents the formation of the earth, 4.6 billion years ago, and the nearest peg represents today. Each of the steps or metres between the two pegs is therefore the equivalent of fifty million years.

Your teacher is now going to give you a card from the Teacher Book (pp.38–39) with information about an event in British history and its date. Officially, history begins with the appearance of written records, written about a place by people living there. In Britain, this coincides with the Roman invasion in AD 54. What you need to do now is to stand in the correct place along the line according to the date of the British historic event on your card, remembering that one metre or step back in time from the 'today peg' is proportional to fifty million years!

'The island is triangular in form and the most civilised of nations are those who inhabit Kent which is entirely a maritime district. All of the Britons indeed, dye themselves with woad, which occasions a bluish colour, and thereby have a more terrible appearance in fight. They wear their hair long and have every part of their body shaved except for the head and upper lip.'

From *Commentarii de Bello Gallico* (AD 54), one of the first written records of British history

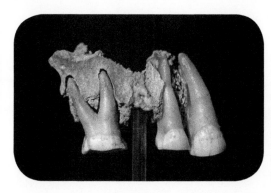

The Kents Cavern, Torquay: human jawbone and the oldest human fossil found in Britain (41,000 years old but only 0.008 mm back along the 100 m timeline)

Almost all of Britain's recorded *history* has been made during the past 2000 years, so on your 100 m timeline this means that all of the events on the cards would have to fit into just the last 0.0004 mm in front of the peg representing today, which is where everyone with a card would have had to stand! Even if we attempt to show *prehistory* in Britain on the timeline, things don't get much easier.

Prehistory, or prehistoric time, is the time from when modern humans first appeared in Britain to the beginning of recorded history. Although the first modern humans evolved in Africa 2.5 million years ago, the earliest evidence of them in Britain is not until 500,000 years ago at Boxgrove in Sussex. However, some archaeologists have dated a more recent discovery of a flint hand axe with a butchered bone in Lynford, Norfolk as 700,000 years old. But even this would only be 0.15 mm back along your 100 m timeline!

> What did you learn from this activity? Why was the activity so difficult to carry out successfully? ▶▶

- Returning to the 100 m timeline marked out on the playground or field, carry out the same exercise as previously but this time use the second set of information cards from the Teacher Book (pp.40–41), which tell you about important events in the life of the earth.

- These have been sourced from the British Geological Survey website at:

  http://www.bgs.ac.uk/ discoveringGeology/time/ timeline/teachers_notes. html

  where further information is available.

- Read the card that you have selected to the rest of the group and then go and stand in the correct place on the timeline according to the date the event occurred.

It has been estimated that the solar system (of which the earth is a part) is about half way through its life – so if it were a person it would be in its mid-forties. In other words, all being well, the earth has at least another 4.6 billion years to go!

Everything that occurred on Earth prior to the beginning of prehistory, approximately 2.5 million years before present (ybp) – which is 99.94% of the planet's life so far – is referred to as geological or *deep time*. The main periods of geological or deep time are shown in the diagram on the first page of this enquiry, although it must be remembered that early modern humans had made an appearance by the Quaternary, which is therefore officially part of prehistory.

4.2 What was the Permian period of deep time like?

The Permian geological period extends from approximately 299 to 251 million ybp. The images on these two pages provide a representation of what geographers believe the Permian environment over most of the earth was like. Geologists analyse rocks, fossils and present day environments to 'reconstruct' what periods of deep time like the Permian were like.

Use these images to write a 100-word (maximum) summary of what you think conditions were like during the Permian. Don't forget to think about the distribution of land; **climate**; vegetation; and the nature of living things.

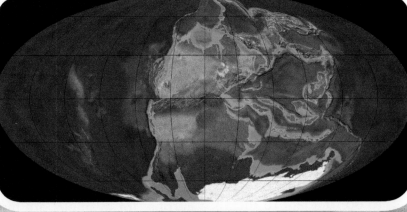

Prof. Iain Stewart, University of Plymouth

- Go to http://www. earthgrind.com/earth-100-million-years-in-future/ and compare maps of present day Earth with that predicted for 100 million years in the future.

- Identify three present-day locations where there will be considerable change.

- What are the changes in these three places going to be?

- What do you think the implications will be for the people currently living at these locations?

- What might they have to do to adapt to the changes?

- Make notes so that you can discuss your ideas.

During the Permian period, the world was dominated by a single supercontinent known as Pangea surrounded by a global ocean known as Panthalassa. At the centre of Pangea, vast regions of **arid** desert formed and reptiles (not dinosaurs) that could better cope with the drier conditions became dominant. Just like in hot deserts today, plants had to adapt to long periods of drought.

The geological record shows that there were rare, violent storms in the desert, which caused flash floods to sweep stones and rock down the dry desert valleys out into surrounding open plains. The water rapidly soaked into the dry rocky and sandy ground, dumping its load of sediments. Slowly the iron within the sediments was oxidised to create the mineral **haematite** and this explains the deep red colour of Permian-age rocks we can see today as far apart as the Mohave Desert in Nevada and Goodrington Beach in the UNESCO English Riviera Global Geopark at Torbay in Devon.

4.3 What happened to the supercontinent of Pangea?

▶ Consolidating your thinking ◀

Look at the short film at https://www.youtube.com/watch?v=uGcDed4xVD4, together with the images below. The first globe shows the world's continents within the single landmass of Pangea during Permian times. The maps of the earth below show an aspect of **tectonic activity** known as **continental drift** from 200 and 50 million years ago.

Continental drift is still occurring today. North America and Europe, for example, are moving away from each other at the rate of about 2.5 cm per year.

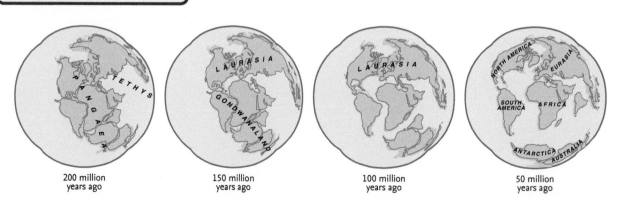

200 million years ago

150 million years ago

100 million years ago

50 million years ago

▶ Consolidating your thinking ◀

Since 2001, UNESCO (United Nations Educational Scientific and Cultural Organisation) has designated sites around the world of particular geologic importance as **Global Geoparks**. The **English Riviera** in Torbay, United Kingdom, is one of just 100 such Global Geoparks in thirty countries around the world. It covers 62 km² of land, 42 km² of sea and 35 km of coastline, covering the three towns of Paignton, Brixham and Torquay.

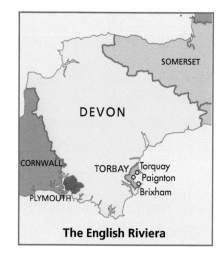

The English Riviera

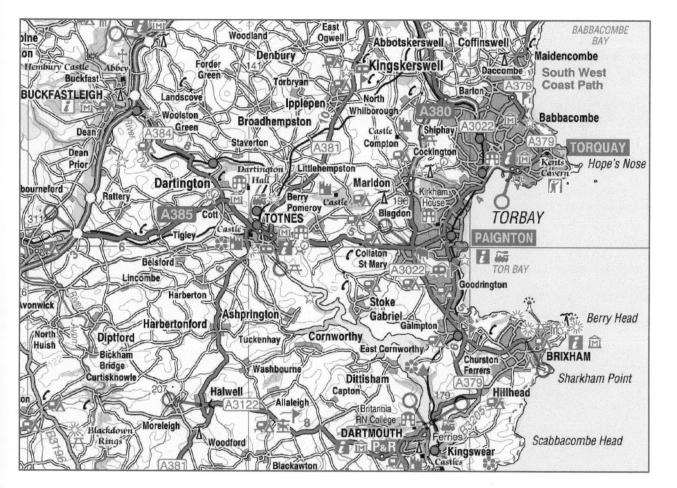

'At first glance, the crowded shores of the English Riviera would seem an unlikely scene to create a Global Geopark. But amid the scattered urban mosaic of Brixham, Paignton and Torquay – tucked away in valleys, on hilltops, along blood-red bluffs or steel-grey sea stacks – is some of the best geology in southern Britain. Who would have thought that rocks laid down in Caribbean coral seas or Saharan desert dunes would now nestle so innocently in the gentle coastal scenery of the English Riviera?'

Professor Iain Stewart,
Plymouth University and BBC television presenter

▶ Consolidating your thinking ◀

Based on the evidence presented on the previous pages, why do you think the English Riviera was designated as a Global Geopark? Discuss your ideas with a partner and then check with the English Riviera Global Geopark website at http://www.englishrivierageopark.org.uk.

The following is an extract from the website:

'The geological tale behind the English Riviera Geopark is quite spectacular and one of extremes. From a seascape bathed in the warm and beautiful tropical seas of the Devonian period to a landscape of arid, barren Permian desert the Geopark's outstanding contribution in terms of the development of geological sciences is astounding.'

There are currently 100 Global Geoparks in thirty member states around the world co-ordinated by the Global Geoparks Network:

http://www. globalgeopark.org/ homepageaux/ tupai/6513.htm

▶▶

Within your group select one Global Geopark each from those around the world, ensuring that locations in as many countries as possible are represented. Then prepare a six-slide PowerPoint presentation to describe and explain the following:

• Key facts about your Global Geopark e.g. its location; size; physical and human characteristics.

• The reasons why it has been designated as a Global Geopark – its geological importance.

• Images of the Global Geopark to illustrate key points you have made.

Early Permian landscape: the first trees began to populate Earth

Katla Geopark, Iceland

About 252 million years ago, at the end of the Permian period, 96% of all living things on Planet Earth died in the worst mass extinction the world has ever seen. All life on Earth today is descended from the 4% of species that survived **Armageddon**. What caused this mass extinction is not certain and geographers have different views as to what led to the Great Dying on Earth.

▶ **Consolidating your thinking** ◀

On this page and the next are a number of images and graphics that provide clues and suggest reasons why the earth almost came to an end 252 million years ago. Analyse all of them very carefully and make a list of anything that you feel could be relevant in helping to find an answer to the mystery. Remember to describe *what* each factor is and explain *why* you think this factor may have contributed to almost exterminating all life on Earth.

Changes in the earth's level of biodiversity during the past 500 million years

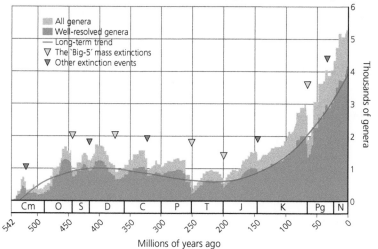

Legend:
- All genera
- Well-resolved genera
- Long-term trend
- ▽ The 'Big-5' mass extinctions
- ▼ Other extinction events

Thousands of genera

Geologic periods:
- Cm Cambrian
- O Ordivician
- S Silurian
- D Devonian
- C Carboniferous
- P Permian
- T Triassic
- J Jurassic
- K Cretaceous
- Pg Paleogene
- N Neogene

Millions of years ago

Oxygen content of Earth's atmosphere

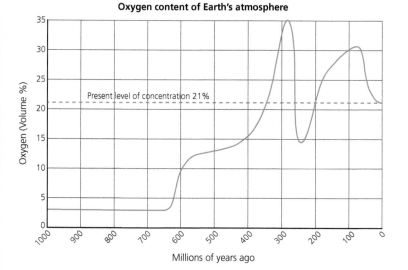

Oxygen (Volume %)

Present level of concentration 21%

Millions of years ago

Average global temperature and proportion of CO_2 in the atmosphere

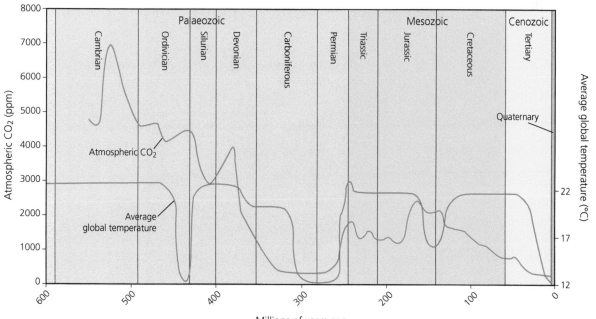

Atmospheric CO_2 (ppm)

Average global temperature (°C)

Palaeozoic — Cambrian, Ordovician, Silurian, Devonian, Carboniferous, Permian
Mesozoic — Triassic, Jurassic, Cretaceous
Cenozoic — Tertiary, Quaternary

Atmospheric CO_2

Average global temperature

Millions of years ago

▶▶

Additional support is available at:

http://environment.
nationalgeographic.com/
environment/global-
warming/acid-rain-
overview/

http://geography.about.
com/od/
globalproblemsandissues/a/
acidrain.htm   ◀◀

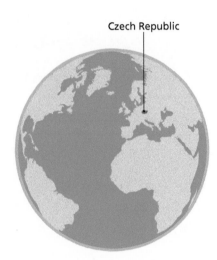

Czech Republic

4.6 Where can we go today to see what the world would have been like after the Permian extinction?

▶ Consolidating your thinking ◀

Read the extract taken from an article by Hillel J. Hoffman that he wrote for the *National Geographic* magazine:

'*"Welcome to the Black Triangle," said paleobiologist Cindy Looy as our van slowed to a stop in the gentle hills of the northern Czech Republic, a few miles from the German and Polish borders. The Black Triangle gets its name from the coal burned by nearby power plants. Decades of acid rain generated by power-plant emissions have devastated the region's ecosystems [...] For months I'd been on the trail of the greatest natural disaster in Earth's history. About 250 million years ago, at the end of the Permian period, something killed some 90 percent of the planet's species. Less than 5 percent of the animal species in the seas survived. On land less than a third of the large animal species made it. Nearly all the trees died. Looy had told me that the Black Triangle was the best place today to see what the world would have looked like after the Permian extinction [...] We saw the first signs of death as we walked into the hills – hundreds of fallen timbers lay hidden in the undergrowth. A forest once grew here. Half a mile uphill we found the trunks of a stand of spruce, killed by acid rain. No birds called, no insects hummed. The only sound was the wind through the acid-tolerant weeds.*'

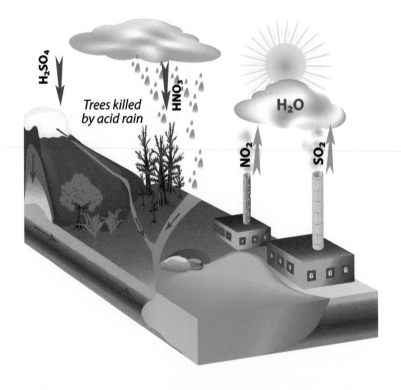

Using the illustration to the right, draw and annotate a flow diagram to show the causes and effects of acid rain in the modern world.

The **acid rain** that is killing forests in places such as the Czech Republic today is, of course, the result of human activity and not natural processes as would have occurred 252 million years ago at the end of the Permian period. But the impact of the acidity on plants and trees is the same.

4.7 Who were the multiple killers of the Permian period?

'Like a homicide detective at a crime scene, Looy sealed the cone in a plastic bag for later lab work. "You could say we're working on the greatest murder mystery of all time," she said. Looy is one of many scientists trying to identify the killer responsible for the largest of the many mass extinctions that have struck the planet [...] But the Permian detectives are faced with a host of suspects and not enough evidence to convict any of them [...] But as Doug Erwin of the Smithsonian cautioned me, "the truth is sometimes untidy." The Permian extinction reminds him of Agatha Christie's Murder on the Orient Express, *in which a corpse with 12 knife wounds is discovered on a train. Twelve different killers conspired to slay the victim. Erwin suspects there may have been multiple killers at the end of the Permian. Maybe everything – eruptions, an impact, anoxia – went wrong at once.'*

Hillel J. Hoffman

► Consolidating your thinking ◄

Think back to the analysis you did of the images on pages 66 and 67, which provided clues about the prime suspects when it comes to finding the guilty party for the mass extinction at the end of the Permian period. Compare your notes with a partner and then contribute your ideas to a whole group discussion.

In March 2014 the *Mail Online* published a story which claimed that methane-producing **microbes** were responsible for the mass extinction at the end of the Permian era.

Read the full story at:

http://www.dailymail.co.uk/sciencetech/article-2593306/Methane-producing-microbes-responsible-Great-Dying.html

How did the release of so much methane by this microbe 'wipe out 90% of species'? Why did so many things die? What geological evidence do the scientists have that this 'belching out' of methane happened 252 million years ago anyway?

The prime suspects for the death of the Permian are:

- an **asteroid** impact on Earth
- massive volcanic eruptions
- climate change
- the build-up of catastrophically high levels of methane and carbon dioxide in the earth's **atmosphere**
- a huge drop in oxygen levels in the ocean.

►►

Geographers are still concerned about methane today because it is one of the most potent greenhouse gases. Have a look at the graphs of major greenhouse gas trends 1975–2015 in the Teacher Book (p.44) and answer the questions provided.

4.8 What caused the microbes to 'belch out' so much methane?

Although there is strong evidence to suggest that the release of so much methane from microbes in the ocean 252 million years ago led to a mass extinction on Earth, **palaeontologists** are still investigating what caused them to do it. The story of the Permian extinction ended with the methane-belching microbes but it began at least a million years before in the land which today we call Siberia, in Russia.

Area of Siberian Traps in northern Russia

:::: Lava ⊟⊟⊟ Tuffe

▶ Consolidating your thinking ◀

The Animal Planet film at https://www.youtube.com/
watch?v=xVz7a8Kkg1Y, called *Animal Armageddon: The
Great Dying*, describes and explains the sequence of events
which led up to the microbes in the ocean producing their
deadly methane, which ultimately wiped out most of life on
Earth 252 million years ago.

The first event in the sequence that led up to the mass
extinction is shown in the section of film from 08.50 to
14.25 mins. This massive sequence of volcanic eruptions
created a feature known as the *Siberian Traps*. Take time to
make notes on a copy of the sequence of events sheet in
the Teacher Book (p.45). In particular, consider which living
things would be most likely to survive? Obviously the larger
and slower reptiles had virtually no chance against the lava
flood. Those that survived had no food left (trees and other
animals, for example) and quickly starved. How might
smaller creatures in the sea have survived? Why would sea
creatures stand more chance?

The next stage in the extinction chain reaction is shown in
the section of the film between 14.25 and 20.29 mins. What
were the two gases that built up in the atmosphere at this
time? What effect did each have? As the planet got warmer,
what element of the atmosphere declined? How did this
affect the animals? What could the small *Thrinaxodon* do
that meant that it survived?

The third incident in the story is covered between 20.30 and
23.18 mins in the film. What began to occur in the earth's
atmosphere and what effect did it have on the
environment? Why was the little *Thrinaxodon* able to
survive once again?

Beginning at 29.29 mins and playing to 33.50 mins, this
section of the film shows the planet 10,000 years after the
extinction began and life is almost extinct. Now the last
stage of the extinction begins with changes in the seas and
oceans. What did the bacteria begin to produce? What
happened to this poison gas? What effect did its release
have on the environment?

> After 1.2 million years,
> the Great Dying on
> Earth began to draw
> to a close and 96% of
> all living things were
> extinct.
>
> But *Thrinaxodon*
> survived. Why was it
> lucky for the human
> race that it did? ▶▶

4.9 How can we represent the great extinction at the end of the Permian period in the Paignton Geoplay Park?

Paignton Geoplay Park, which is situated within the English Riviera Global Geopark, has been designed around the incredible geological history of the area and, in particular, the four geological periods of the *Devonian*, *Permian*, *Carboniferous* and *Quaternary*. It is amazingly popular and enjoyed every day of the year by tens of thousands of children who either live locally or are visiting Torbay on holiday from other parts of the UK and overseas.

Within the Geoplay Park, the hot desert environment of the Permian period is represented by large areas of sand with digging equipment that the children can operate, together with channels down which the children can send torrents of water to create the effects of flash flooding. Then there are the carved giant millipedes, which appear all around the Permian zone to remind children of what was alive in and around Torbay 252 million years ago!

Applying your skills

The English Riviera Global Geopark has decided to run a competition for the design and construction of two additions to their Geoplay Park in Paignton:

- Firstly, it wants a new piece of play equipment for the Permian zone of the Geoplay Park to represent the extinction event that would have occurred there 252 million years ago. This piece of equipment needs to be attractive to the children and fun to play on as well as telling the story behind the Great Dying. For example, it could include *Thrinaxodon* somewhere!

- Secondly, it wants a new interpretation board, like the one opposite, for parents and carers who come to the play park with their children. This needs to tell the story of the four stages in the Great Dying and the importance of the survival of *Thrinaxodon*. Remember that this will be for older people and can therefore include more detail but nevertheless will still need to be visually attractive to gain people's attention. You will need to balance text and visual images carefully.

You now need to generate a *design brief* to include the chosen layout, dimensions and any patterns, colours, particular shapes and materials to be used to make each of your commissions. Each will also include a simple explanation of how the design is conveying the key messages of the extinction event. How can we help children and adults to learn through what we are making and invite them to play on, look at or read about? How can we create a design for a model, sculpture, picture or piece of play equipment that tells people about the four things that happened, which almost ended life for ever? How can they all be incorporated into one design?

At the end of the design process you will be asked to make a presentation of your brief to explain why you have designed the products the way you have.

Be prepared to say which aspects of your design and model you are most pleased with, any changes you made from your original design and how these alterations improved the outcome.

5 Disasters and risky places

Are Haiti and the Philippines risky places to live?

There are now over seven billion humans on Planet Earth and this number is expected to rise above nine billion by 2050. Increasingly, people are living in places where they face many risks and in lots of these places the risks are growing. Many countries are struggling to cope with rapidly expanding populations and **migration** into cities.

Over 50% of humans now live in **urban environments** and it can be very challenging to develop the **infrastructure** (including roads, power, water, waste disposal, etc.) fast enough to support the growing population.

Because of increasing populations many of these places are also located in hazard zones where the people could be at risk from one or even multiple hazards (such as volcanic eruptions, hurricanes, **earthquakes**, floods, landslides, tsunamis, etc.) and the number of recorded natural disasters is increasing. Add all of these factors together and you have a rising number of risky places to live.

▶ Consolidating your thinking ◀

Look at the images on these two pages. Use these and *your own knowledge and understanding* to build up a concept map around the central question 'What makes a place risky to live in?' In a concept map each word or phrase connects to another and links back to the original idea, word or phrase – in this case *risky places*. These images are just a starting point. You will have many other ideas.

Did you know?

Hazard or disaster?

A hazard is a natural event that has the potential to cause damage, loss of life and disruption, whereas a disaster occurs when the hazard interacts with people. How big a disaster depends on many factors. A hurricane that passes over an uninhabited island is a hazard not a disaster.

▶▶

Did you know?

To be recorded as a disaster in the database, one of the following conditions must be met:

- Ten or more people reported killed

- 100 or more people reported affected

- Declaration of a state of emergency

- Call for international assistance

Figure A: *Earthquake smartphone app with real time Tweets*

Try some real time earthquake tracking by downloading a smartphone app or checking out the United States Geological Survey at:

http://earthquake.usgs.gov/earthquakes/map/

5.2 Is the world experiencing more disasters?

A key part of establishing whether places are risky to live in is to examine global trends in disasters. The EM-DAT Disaster Database has been collating data on disasters dating back to the year 1900. There are some interesting trends and patterns that emerge when we look at the data graphically.

▶ Consolidating your thinking ◀

Examine the four graphs on these pages. What is the general trend shown in each of the sets of data in the graphs? What could be responsible for each of the trends you have identified? Consider the impact that a rising global population, improvements in recording and reporting, climate change and the role of technology and communication (such as the Internet and **smartphone** apps like Earthquake shown in Figure A) could have had. Write your analysis on the sheets provided in the Teacher Book (pp.48–51).

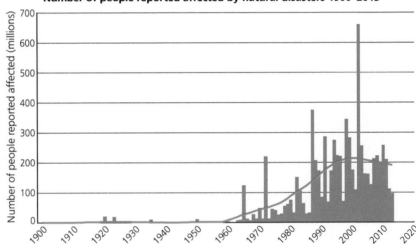

Number of people reported affected by natural disasters 1900–2013

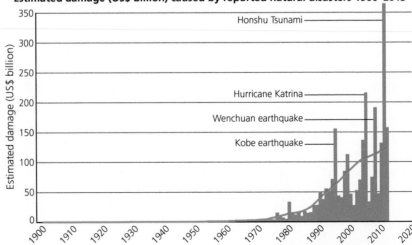

Estimated damage (US$ billion) caused by reported natural disasters 1900–2013

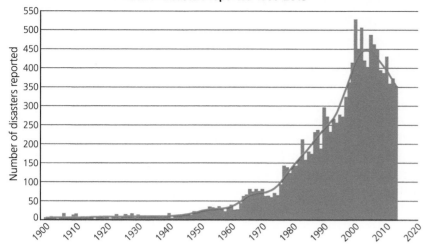

Natural disasters reported 1900–2013

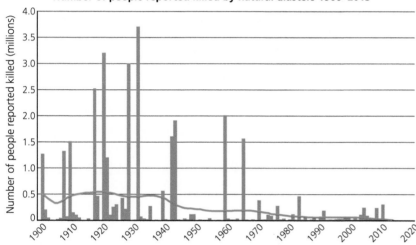

Number of people reported killed by natural diasters 1900–2013

Extending your enquiry ▶▶

Which disasters have been reported more frequently since 1900? Which have been reported less frequently?

Use the Internet to compile a list of disasters that have occurred globally from 2012 onwards. Does the data you have compiled confirm or contradict the patterns you identified from the graphs above? If not, can you suggest reasons why this might be the case?

5.3 What factors affect risk and vulnerability to disasters?

Globally, from 2002 to 2011 there were an average of 394 disasters each year around the world, which killed an average of 107,000 people annually in total. The mean number of people affected by these disasters each year was 268 million and they cost US$143 billion in economic damages. However, these impacts were not evenly spread across the planet and some places are more likely than others to have higher numbers of fatalities and victims.

In some places, smaller earthquakes will do substantially more damage and kill many more people than much stronger earthquakes elsewhere. The same is true for **tropical cyclones** (storms), where similar scale events in different parts of the world will have substantially different outcomes. Why do you think this is?

▶ Consolidating your thinking ◀

Working with a partner, make a list of all the reasons why two earthquakes of similar magnitude or two hurricanes of similar strength might have very different consequences depending on where they occur in the world.

For any place in the world there are three important concepts or general ideas to consider when thinking about the risk from a hazard:

• Probability – how likely it is that a hazard will occur

• Vulnerability – how exposed the people are in an area to the effects of a hazard

• The ability of people to cope – before, during and after the disaster.

For example, Florida, USA has a high probability that hurricanes will occur, but the people there are less vulnerable due to advanced warning systems, education programmes, building codes, compulsory storm insurance, evacuations and disaster management plans. They have a good ability to cope with hurricanes so overall risk is lowered, but importantly not eliminated. A hazard here could still become a disaster, but on a smaller scale than if the same event were to hit the Philippines, for example.

Buildings designed to withstand earthquakes

▶ Consolidating your thinking ◀

You are now going to investigate the factors that affect vulnerability and the ability to cope with disasters to see if you can explain why some places are more seriously affected by hazards than others.

Examine the range of factors shown in the spider diagram below that affect risk and vulnerability to hazards. It is key that you recognise that not all hazards become disasters and that it is not simply the size of the physical event that determines the impact of a disaster but a complex, interlinked series of human factors.

Spend two minutes thinking about each of the factors. Then, with a partner, discuss how each of the factors could impact on how vulnerable people are and how at risk this makes them. You could split the factors into different categories and you should consider how the factors could increase or decrease vulnerability. Finally, discuss your ideas with another pair. You should then aim to write about the influence of three factors in detail.

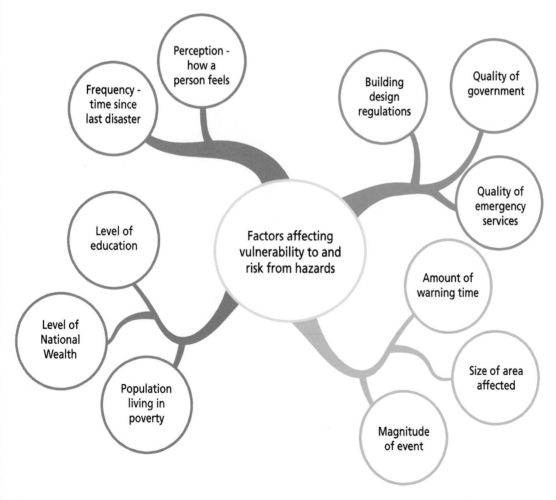

Applying your skills

Examine the images carefully. For each one identify any factors that increase or decrease vulnerability.

5.4 Why are the Philippines and Haiti risky places to live?

You should by now have a good understanding of the patterns and trends in disasters and the concepts of *risk* and *vulnerability*. Two countries you are likely to have heard of are the Philippines and Haiti. These countries have suffered from natural disasters in recent years that have had devastating effects with huge loss of life. You will need to use the country profiles on the following pages to begin building a clear picture of why these countries are so badly affected by disasters. Each profile contains a range of statistics, maps, photographs and a section focusing on a recent disaster.

▶ Consolidating your thinking ◀

Individually, you will need to use the information on the following pages and the framework provided in the Teacher Book (p.52) to collect data on both countries and the factors that contribute to risk and vulnerability. In particular, you will be challenged to work out an answer to the question: *Why do hazards in these places become disasters?*

You will then need to work with a small group to produce an outcome piece of work that demonstrates your skills, knowledge and understanding of disasters and risky places. This work has to focus on either the Philippines or Haiti.

Your work will have to give a background of the country and then move on to examine the factors causing vulnerability and increased risk here. Finally, you will need to investigate a specific disaster event.

There is further guidance for you in the Teacher Book (p.53) as well as suggestions for ways of presenting your work.

Extending your enquiry ⟩⟩

Make use of Google Earth layers to create hazard maps. You can easily create image overlays to show population density, earthquake shake maps, damage maps, etc. First save the image to your computer, select 'Add' in the menu bar and then click 'Image overlay'.

Haiti factfile

Brief history	A former French colony that declared independence in 1804. Haiti has suffered from political instability and is currently the poorest country in the western hemisphere.
Area	27,750 km²
Population	9,996,731 (July 2014 est.)
Population density	360 people per km²
Population growth rate	1.08%
Infant mortality rate	49.43 deaths per 1000 live births
Life expectancy at birth	63.18 years
Adult literacy rate	48.7%
Number of hospital beds	1.3 beds per 1000 population (2007)
% of population with access to improved drinking water	64%
Risk from major infectious diseases	High
GDP per capita	US$1300 (2013 est.)
GDP growth rate	3.4% (2013 est.)

Top five natural disasters in Haiti by mortality (1994–2010)

Date	Disaster type	Persons killed	Persons affected
January 2010	Earthquake	222,570	3,700,000
September 2004	Storm (Tropical Cyclone Jeanne)	2754	315,594
May–June 2004	Flood	2665	31,283
November 1994	Storm (Tropical Cyclone Gordon)	1122	1,587,000
September 2008	Storm (Tropical Cyclone Hanna)	529	48,000

Source: EM-DAT International Disaster Database

> Previous earthquake occurrence in Haiti: 27 October 1952 – six persons reported killed ▶▶

Haiti Earthquake
January 2010

The Richter Scale

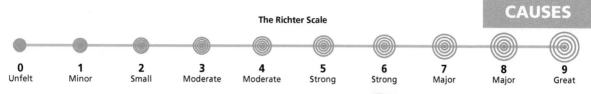

0	1	2	3	4	5	6	7	8	9
Unfelt	Minor	Small	Moderate	Moderate	Strong	Strong	Major	Major	Great

 16:53:10 local time

 7 on the Richter Scale

 15 km SW of Port-au-Prince

 Depth of **10 km**

 Over **3.5** million people experienced strong to extreme shaking

 52 strong aftershocks in the 12 days after the main earthquake

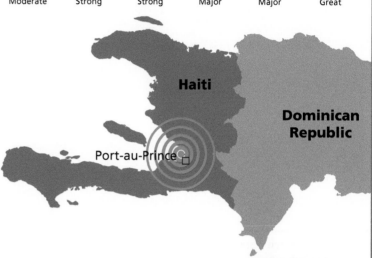

Haiti

Dominican Republic

Port-au-Prince

Damage

 300 000 injured people

222 570 deaths

19 million cubic metres of rubble and debris

 105 000 houses destroyed

188 383 houses damaged

4000 schools were damaged or destroyed

The Presidential Palace collapsed along with 3 hospitals, the main prison and the United Nations HQ.

The main port was so severely damaged that ships carrying aid could not dock.

An outbreak of cholera occurred in October 2010. By July 2011,

5899

people had died as a result of the outbreak and 216,000 were infected.

Responses

A lack of rescue equipment meant survivors dug at the rubble with bare hands to free those trapped.

Help from USA

 Over **600 000** people left their homes in Port-au-Prince

 1.5 million people were living in camps

12 fixed-wing aircraft

 48 helicopters

 17 ships

International aid

 Over **3.5** billion dollars was raised

 532 440 bottles of water

 111 082 meals

 **4100 kg** medical supplies

Haiti risk factors

Map of Haiti storm tracks

North American Plate

Caribbean Plate

DOMINICAN REPUBLIC

HAITI

Port-au-Prince

Baracoa
Maisí
Jauco
Le Môle St Nicolas
Port-de-Paix
Monte Cristi
Luperón
Puerto Plata
Cap-Haïtien
Fort Liberté
Gonaïves
St Michel de l'Atalaye
Santiago
Moca
La Vega
St Marc
Hinche
Elías Piña
Verrettes
San Juan
Bonao
Dame Marie
Jérémie
Mirebalais
Petit-Goâve
Jimani
Neiba
Azua
Port-à-Piment
Les Cayes
Bainet
Jacmel
Saltrou
Duvergé
Barahona
Baní
San Pedro de Macoris
La Romana
Santo Domingo
Pedernales
Enriquillo

Population density

Persons per sq km

	over 2500
	1000–2500
	500–1000
	250–500
	100–250
	less than 100

Port-de-Paix
Cap-Haïtien
Gonaïves
Jérémie
Port-au-Prince
Les Cayes
Jacmel

- – – North American plate line
- – – Subduction zones
- – – Transform faults
- ☆ Haiti earthquake
- ⬤ Other earthquake epicentres

Philippines factfile

Brief history	A former Spanish colony that came under US control after a war in 1898. In 1935, the Philippines became a self-governing commonwealth, but it was invaded by Japan in 1942. After WWII, the country declared independence. The USA closed its last military base in 1992.		
Area	300,000 km²	**Population growth rate**	1.81% (2014 est.)
Population	107,668,231	**Infant mortality rate**	17.64 deaths per 1000 live births
Population density	359 people per km²	**Life expectancy at birth**	72.48 years
Adult literacy rate	95.4%	**Risk from major infectious diseases**	High
Number of hospital beds	1 bed per 1000 population (2011)	**GDP per capita**	US$4700 (2013 est.)
% of population with access to improved drinking water	92.4%	**GDP growth rate**	6.8% (2013 est.)

Top five natural disasters in the Philippines by mortality (1976–2013)

Date	Disaster type	Persons killed
November 2013	Storm (Tropical Cyclone Haiyan)	7986
August 1976	Earthquake	6000
November 1991	Storm (Tropical Cyclone Thelma)	5956
July 1990	Earthquake	2412
December 2012	Storm (Tropical Cyclone Bopha)	1901

Source: EM-DAT International Disaster Database

Top five natural disasters in the Philippines by persons affected (1990–2013)

Date	Disaster type	Persons affected
November 2013	Storm (Tropical Cyclone Haiyan)	16,106,807
December 2012	Storm (Tropical Cyclone Bopha)	6,246,664
November 1990	Storm (Tropical Cyclone Mike)	6,159,569
September 2009	Storm (Tropical Cyclone Ondoy)	4,901,763
June 2008	Storm (Tropical Cyclone Fengsheng)	4,785,460

Source: EM-DAT International Disaster Database

The Philippines Typhoon Haiyan/Yolanda
November 2013

Saffir Simpson Scale

1	2	3	4	5
Very dangerous 119–153 km/h	Extremely dangerous 154–177 km/h	Devastating damage 178–208 km/h	Catastrophic damage 209–251 km/h	Catastrophic damage 252 + km/h

Samar Island

The Philippines

The Philippines are made up of over **7000** islands

Typhoon Haiyan

Haiyan was the **25th** tropical storm to enter Filipino waters in 2013

It caused a **7.6** metre-high storm surge

Samar Island

Typhoon Haiyan hit eastern Samar Island at **4:40** a.m. on 8 November

Sustained winds of **237** km per hour

Gusts of **275** km per hour

EFFECTS

The city of Tacloban suffered catastrophic damage:

Over **6000** deaths

4.1 million displaced people

5.6 million people in need of food aid

1.1 million homes were damaged or destroyed

Over **14.1** million people were affected across 46 provinces

RESPONSES

4 million people given food assistance

500 000 households received basic emergency shelter materials

97 000 children were screened for malnutrition

420 000 children received temporary educational materials

The Philippines risk factors

Map of the Philippines storm tracks

Map legend
- International boundary
- Plate line
- Storm track
- Volcano
- Earthquake epicentre

Eurasian Plate
Pacific Plate
Philippine Sea Plate
Australian Plate

Luzon Strait
PACIFIC OCEAN
Luzon
Cabanatuan
Manila
Quezon City
Lucena
Batangas
Catanduanes
Mindoro
South China Sea
Samar
PHILIPPINES
Panay
Tacloban
Bacolod
Cebu
Negros
Butuan
Palawan
Mindanao
Pagadian
Davao
Sulu Sea
General Santos
Sulu Archipelago
Celebes Sea
Kepulauan Talaud

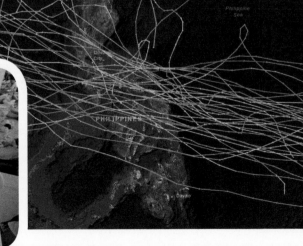

Remember that the number of people affected by disasters around the world is increasing and that the number of weather-related hazards has grown at the fastest rate.

▶▶

You should hopefully now have a clear understanding of the factors that affect vulnerability to hazards and how many of these factors combined with deadly effect in either Haiti or the Philippines.

▶ **Consolidating your thinking** ◀

Look carefully at Figure A. It is a photograph of Teresita Tenorio and her children. They lived in Alang Alang, eleven miles inland and west of Tacloban City in the Philippines. On 8 November 2013, Typhoon Haiyan tore through Leyte Island and devastated the community in their small town. The Google crisis map produced after the typhoon classified this area as 'destroyed'. With no power or communication, none of their family knew of their fate. One relative posted a message for them on *Google Person Finder*, but received no answer.

How can we reduce the risks from these natural hazards and minimise the scale of the disaster? Tropical storms like Typhoon Haiyan are unstoppable, but it is possible to reduce the vulnerability of people before, during and after these events.

▶▶

Figure A

The tragic story of the Tenorio family should focus your minds on developing strategies or products to reduce the vulnerability of families like theirs to typhoons, earthquakes and other similar disasters.

▶▶

When the storm surge hit, Teresita, her eldest son and her youngest daughter died in their house, crushed by debris and swept away. The bodies of the children were found on the edge of the town. Teresita is still classified as 'missing'.

Her other two children survived. Amid the chaos, they struggled to find food and to avoid looters. Eleven people died nearby when a wall collapsed as desperate people raided a rice warehouse. The children survived for one week on whatever they could, until outside help arrived. They are now living in Manila with relatives.

► Consolidating your thinking ◄

In places like Tacloban City in the Philippines and Port-au-Prince in Haiti, countless lives could be saved by developing methods of reducing vulnerability with **appropriate technology**.

Your final task in this enquiry is to design a product that can save lives in disaster zones either before, during or after the event. You will need to convince the United Nations International Strategy for Disaster Reduction (UNISDR) to buy your product and send it to people to use in risky places around the world. Your focus has to be on designing a simple way of reducing the factors that make people vulnerable. There are several key stages in the design process:

- Develop a mind map of your ideas – be creative!

- Choose one or two other people to work with and pool all of your ideas.

- Practical Action is a charity which seeks to help poor people around the world to use appropriate technology to reduce their vulnerability and to cope with natural disasters. You might gain inspiration for your own invention from the kind of projects that Practical Action has been involved with at:

  http://practicalaction.org/reducing-vulnerability

- Decide on your favourite idea. Remember, it will need to be low-cost as you are developing this for people with very little income.

- Draw annotated designs to describe and explain how your product will work.

- You could build a 3D model in *SketchUp* or a similar programme or build a prototype out of a range of materials. Remember to keep product costs low. You could even consider using recycled materials.

- Write a 'sales pitch'. Your team will need to use persuasive language to prepare a pitch that convinces the United Nations to choose your product. You could also prepare a presentation.

- You will have to score the presentations from other groups in order to decide which is the most effective product.

- Your teacher will provide you with some guidance on writing and a peer assessment sheet from the Teacher Book (pp.54–55).

6 Don't snatch!

How is so-called 'land grabbing' affecting Africa?

'There's a new scramble for land in Africa and it's going on at an incredible rate.'

Alex Wijeratna (2014),
Action Aid (UK Development Agency)

6.1 What happened during the first 'scramble for Africa'?

▶ Consolidating your thinking ◀

All of the maps and images on this page and the previous page provide clues as to what happened in Africa about 130 years ago. The *'scramble'* as it is referred to involved several powerful European countries. What do you think went on during the *'scramble'* and why?

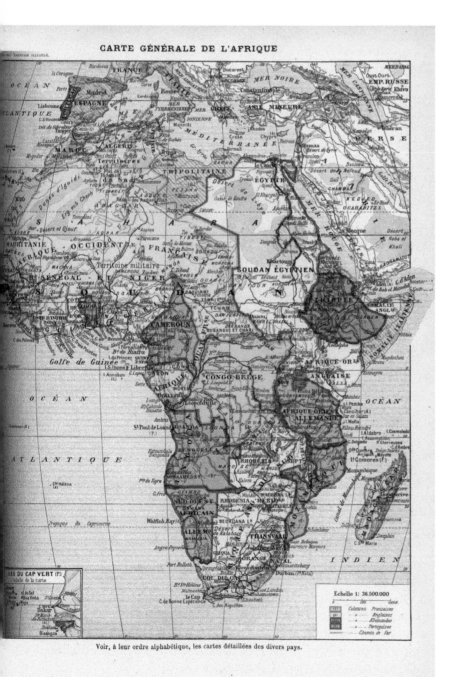

The term *'scramble for Africa'* refers to the period between 1880 and 1912 when rival European powers used their wealth, considerable military might and developing technology to conquer very large areas of the African continent. Occupied territories became **colonies** of the European countries that took control of them. At a conference in Berlin in 1884, the European powers met to divide up the continent of Africa between them – a process one observer referred to as 'cutting up the African cake'.

As the map of Africa below shows, by 1912 all of the continent was occupied by one or other of the European powers. British possessions are shown in pink; French in dark blue; Belgian in yellow; German in light blue; Portuguese in purple; Italian in green and Spanish in lilac. Only Ethiopia and Liberia remained independent (white).

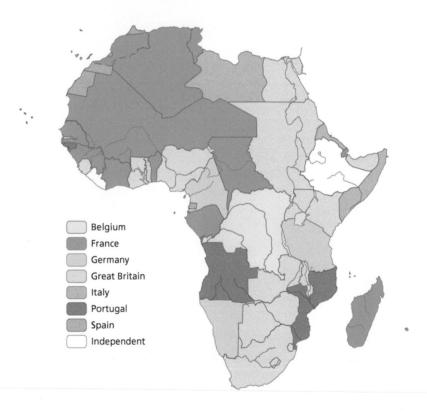

Belgium
France
Germany
Great Britain
Italy
Portugal
Spain
Independent

One of the most important reasons for European countries to have colonies in Africa was to obtain **raw materials** that they did not possess themselves. One such resource was agricultural produce that required semi-tropical or tropical climates to grow, such as tea, coffee, cotton, tobacco, sugar cane, rubber, palm oil, bananas and cacao. European governments supported farmers to obtain the most fertile farmland in their colonies and to set up **plantations** on which to grow the products that could then be exported back to consumers in 'the mother country'.

Food is essential to human survival and the price of the food we need has seen a massive increase in the past decade.

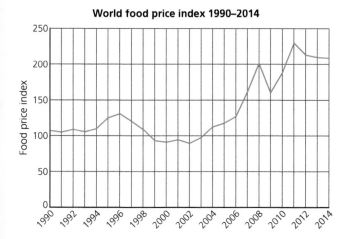

World food price index 1990–2014

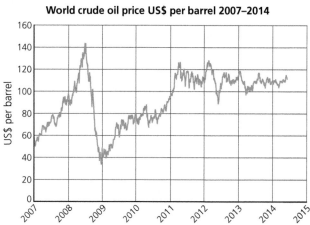

World crude oil price US$ per barrel 2007–2014

▶ Consolidating your thinking ◀

Geographers do not think that population growth is to blame for the increase in the price of food. They point to the fact that even though the world's population has grown from 1.6 billion in 1900 to over seven billion today, during this time the annual rate of growth in grain production has always been greater than yearly world population growth. The increase in global food production has kept pace with the increase in the number of people living in the world.

The following five factors are considered to be a more likely cause of the rapid increase in world food prices. Consider each one and try to work out how it could have contributed to pushing prices up.

1. Rising crude oil prices

Remember that **crude oil** is refined to make petrol and diesel to power vehicles and machinery as well as to produce important chemicals such as ammonia and phosphates used in fertilisers.

Working with a partner, describe the overall trend in world food prices shown in the graph above.

Now discuss what might have caused the price of food to 'spike' the way it did on the graph in 2008–2009 and 2011–2012? This led, for example, to the average world prices for rice rising by 217%; wheat by 136%; maize by 125% and soybeans by 107%.

Think about possible natural and human events which might have led to these steep increases in the price of food.

2. Increasing cost of chemical fertilisers

Fertiliser prices (US$ per ton)

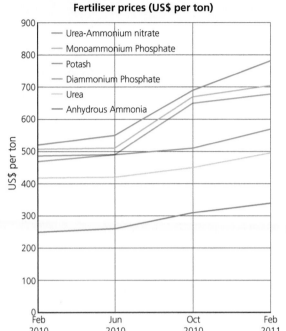

Legend:
- Urea-Ammonium nitrate
- Monoammonium Phosphate
- Potash
- Diammonium Phosphate
- Urea
- Anhydrous Ammonia

Y-axis: US$ per ton (0 to 900)

X-axis: Feb 2010, Jun 2010, Oct 2010, Feb 2011

3. Using food crops such as maize to produce biofuels

Biofuels, such as **ethanol,** are used as additives to traditional oil-based motor fuels, such as petroleum, and help to reduce **greenhouse gas** emissions. Currently it is estimated that each year 100 million tonnes of grain (5% of the global harvest) is used to produce biofuels. This percentage is increasing.

Biofuel production 1990–2035

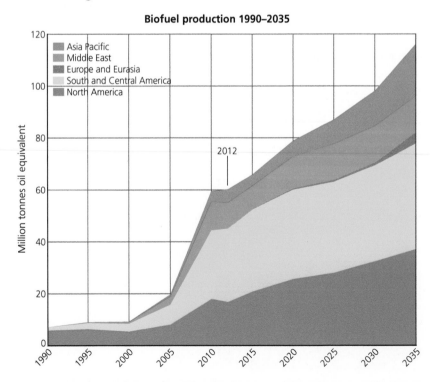

Legend:
- Asia Pacific
- Middle East
- Europe and Eurasia
- South and Central America
- North America

Y-axis: Million tonnes oil equivalent (0 to 120)

X-axis: 1990, 1995, 2000, 2005, 2010, 2015, 2020, 2025, 2030, 2035

2012

4. Extreme weather events around the world

For example, the prolonged **drought** which occurred in and around the Murray–Darling Basin in southern Australia between 2007 and 2012 and directly caused a 98% drop in the country's rice harvest. To think about the implications of events such as these for food prices in a country like Australia, which is the second largest exporter of wheat after the United States, you will need to read the article 'Australia's Long Drought Withering Wheat, Rice Supplies' from *National Geographic News* by Carolyn Barry, which is included in the Teacher Book (p.58).

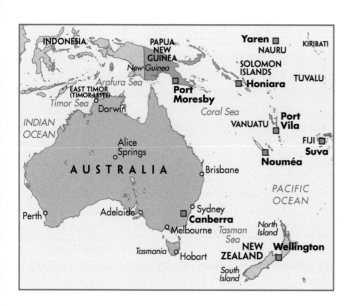

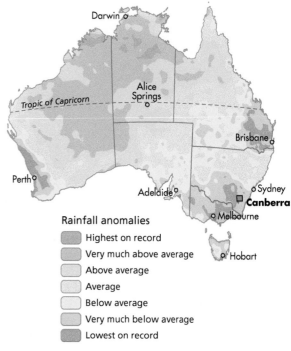

Rainfall anomalies

- Highest on record
- Very much above average
- Above average
- Average
- Below average
- Very much below average
- Lowest on record

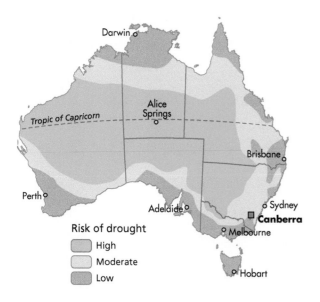

Risk of drought

- High
- Moderate
- Low

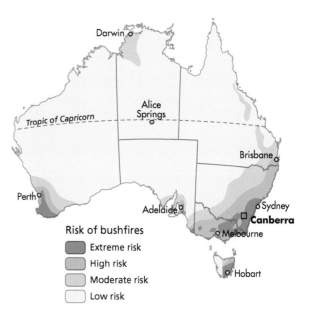

Risk of bushfires

- Extreme risk
- High risk
- Moderate risk
- Low risk

5. Changing diets amongst people in newly prosperous nations

This includes India and China where many people are adopting a more 'western' diet and eating habits, which include consuming more processed foods and meat in general.

In her short article for *The Telegraph* newspaper, 'China's changing eating habits' (available from the Teacher Book on p.59), Bee Wilson considers one effect of changing eating habits in China.

In addition to this, what do you think the effect of changing eating habits has been on world food prices? It's worth reflecting that the production of 1 kg of beef requires 7 kg of grain feed and uses twelve times the amount of water needed to produce 1 kg of wheat and more than five times the amount of land.

The blog post by Richard King of *Oxfam GB* on page 60 of the Teacher Book called 'Global food crisis: The challenges of changing diets' considers other impacts of changing diets around the world. How are changing diets impacting on the environment and how does he think people in wealthier nations can help combat the problem by 'looking long and hard at the contents of our own fridges and dustbins'?

RUSSIA

TURKEY
CYPRUS
LEBANON
ISRAEL
JORDAN
SYRIA
IRAQ
KUWAIT
GEORGIA
ARMENIA
AZERBAIJAN
KAZAKHSTAN
MONGOLIA
N. KOREA
S. KOREA
JAPAN

SAUDI
ARABIA
IRAN
UZBEKISTAN
TURKMENISTAN
KYRGYZSTAN
TAJIKISTAN
AFGHANISTAN
BAHRAIN
QATAR
PAKISTAN
CHINA

UNITED ARAB
EMIRATES
YEMEN
OMAN
NEPAL
BHUTAN
BANGLADESH
TAIWAN

INDIA
MYANMAR
(BURMA)
LAOS
THAILAND
CAMBODIA
VIETNAM
PHILIPPINES

SRI LANKA
BRUNEI
MALAYSIA
SINGAPORE
INDONESIA
EAST TIMOR

A mind map is a very good way of helping you to see how all of the different bits of information fit together and the connections between them. It also helps you to remember information and is a useful revision technique when preparing for examinations.

As an example to help you get going, have a look at the mind map for tourism below and also a simple instructional video produced by MacGrercy Consultants on **YouTube** at:

https://www.youtube.com/watch?v=wLWV0XN7K1g&noredirect=1

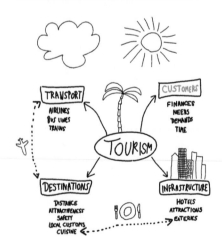

▶ Consolidating your thinking ◀

Before moving on with your investigation of 'land grabbing', devote some time to constructing a *mind map* to summarise what you have learned about why world food prices have risen in recent years.

What to do:

- In the centre of an A3 piece of plain paper write the title *increasing world food prices* and draw a circle around it.

- Draw a line out from the circle for each of the things that are influencing world food prices and write its name along the line, e.g. *biofuel production*.

- At the end of each secondary line draw shorter lines branching out with key facts, phrases and ideas, e.g. *manufacturing etholene from maize; reduced greenhouse gas emissions; mixed with petroleum and gasoline in motor engines*, etc.

- You might also find it useful to use different colours for each secondary line and associated information as well as symbols and images which can be used sometimes instead of words – providing of course you remember later on what they mean!

6.3 How is 'land grabbing' connected to rising food prices?

Since 2008, millions of hectares of land have been bought or **leased** from governments in African nations by foreign companies or organisations based in countries such as Saudi Arabia, the United Arab Emirates, China and India. The American based *Oakland Institute* says that this so-called 'land grabbing' in Africa already totals sixty million hectares – an area the size of France. The advantage for the countries acquiring the land is that they can meet the food demands of their growing populations at home as well as protect themselves from some of the effects of rising global food prices. The United Nations Food and Agricultural Organisation estimates that in the last ten years alone global food prices have risen by 83%.

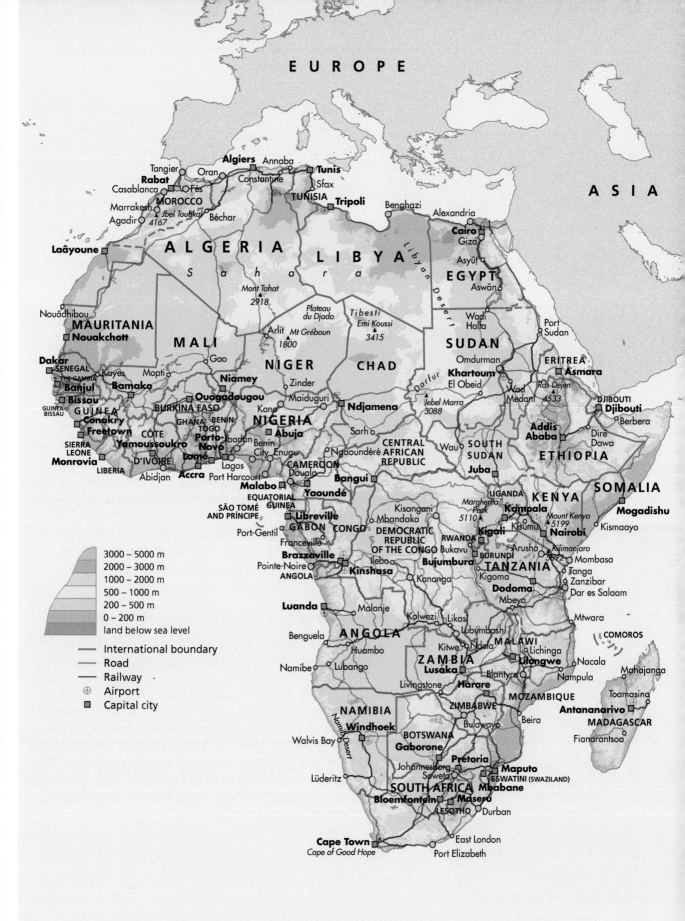

EUROPE

ASIA

Tangier
Rabat
Casablanca
Marrakesh
Agadir
Laâyoune
Nouâdhibou

Algiers   Annaba
Oran   Constantine   Tunis
Fès   Sfax
MOROCCO   TUNISIA   Tripoli
Jbel Toubkal   Béchar
4167

Benghazi   Alexandria
Cairo
Giza
ALGERIA   LIBYA   Asyût
EGYPT
Aswân

Sahara   Libyan Desert

Wadi
Halfa   Port
Sudan

MAURITANIA   MALI
Nouakchott

Mont Tahat
2918

Plateau
du Djado   Tibesti
Arlit   Mt Gréboun   Emi Koussi
1800   3415

NIGER   CHAD   SUDAN
Gao   Omdurman
Dakar   Kayes   Mopti   Khartoum
SENEGAL   Niamey   Zinder   El Obeid
THE GAMBIA   Bamako   Ouagadougou   Maiduguri   Ndjamena   Jebel Marra
Banjul   BURKINA FASO   Kano   3088
Bissau   GUINEA   GHANA   BENIN   NIGERIA   Sarh
GUINEA-   Conakry   TOGO   Abuja   Ngaoundéré   CENTRAL
BISSAU   Freetown   Porto-   Ibadan   Benin   AFRICAN
SIERRA   Yamoussoukro   Novo   City   Enugu   CAMEROON   REPUBLIC
LEONE   CÔTE   Lome   Lagos   Douala   Bangui
Monrovia   D'IVOIRE   Accra   Port Harcourt   Yaoundé
LIBERIA   Abidjan   Malabo
EQUATORIAL   SÃO TOMÉ   GUINEA
AND PRÍNCIPE   Libreville
Port-Gentil   GABON   CONGO
Franceville
Brazzaville
Pointe-Noire   Kinshasa
ANGOLA

Eritrea
Asmara
ERITREA   DJIBOUTI
Ras Dejen   Djibouti
Wad   4533
Medani   Berbera
Addis   Dire
Ababa   Dawa
ETHIOPIA   SOMALIA

Darfur

SOUTH
SUDAN
Wau   Juba

Kisangani
Mbandaka   Margherita   UGANDA
Peak   Kampala   KENYA   Mogadishu
DEMOCRATIC   5110   Kisumu   Mount Kenya
REPUBLIC   RWANDA   Kigali   5199   Nairobi   Kismaayo
OF THE CONGO   Bukavu   BURUNDI   Arusha   Mombasa
Ilebo   Bujumbura   Kilimanjaro
Kananga   Kigoma   5892   Tanga
TANZANIA   Zanzibar
Dodoma   Dar es Salaam

Luanda   Malanje   Mbeya   Mtwara
Kolwezi   Likasi
Benguela   ANGOLA   Lubumbashi   COMOROS
Huambo   Kitwe   Ndola   MALAWI
Namibe   Lubango   ZAMBIA   Lichinga   Nacala
Lusaka   Lilongwe   Mahajanga
Livingstone   Harare   Blantyre   Nampula
ZIMBABWE   MOZAMBIQUE
Beira   Toamasina
NAMIBIA   Antananarivo
Windhoek   Bulawayo   MADAGASCAR
Fianarantsoa
Walvis Bay   BOTSWANA
Gaborone
Pretoria   Maputo
Johannesburg   ESWATINI (SWAZILAND)
Lüderitz   Soweto   Mbabane
SOUTH AFRICA
Bloemfontein   Maseru
LESOTHO   Durban

Cape Town   East London
Cape of Good Hope   Port Elizabeth

3000 – 5000 m
2000 – 3000 m
1000 – 2000 m
500 – 1000 m
200 – 500 m
0 – 200 m
land below sea level

International boundary
Road
Railway
⊕ Airport
■ Capital city

African nations with most land grabbed by foreign companies and government agencies

Country	Land acquired by foreign investors (hectares)
Democratic Republic of Congo	8,250,310
Sudan	3,281,429
Tanzania	1,917,749
Mozambique	1,496,935
South Sudan	1,408,500
Ethiopia	1,001,382
Uganda	858,870
Morocco	700,000

Country	Land acquired by foreign investors (hectares)
Republic of Congo	664,000
Liberia	649,800
Sierra Leone	423,550
Gabon	407,200
Madagascar	369,100
Nigeria	362,292
Cameroon	294,960

▶ **Consolidating your thinking** ◀

Using the outline political map of Africa from the Teacher Book (p.79), draw located vertical proportional bars to show these statistics for each country shown in the table. Add a scale. Looking at your completed map, discuss with a partner any spatial patterns in the data you observe. For example, are some geographical areas of Africa more represented than others? If so, why might this be? Are there any exceptions to the general pattern?

6.4 What are the costs and benefits of land grabbing in Africa?

Ethiopia, under the leadership of Prime Minister Meles Zenawi, has agreed 815 land leasing projects with overseas countries since 2007. The majority of these deals involve land in the more fertile areas of the west and south of the country, such as the Gambella region, which is comparable in size to Belgium. In his book, *The Landgrabbers: The New Fight over Who Owns the Earth*, Fred Pearce describes his first impressions of Gambella:

'Gambella is the poorest province in one of the world's poorest nations – a lowland appendix in the far south-west of Ethiopia. Geographically and ethnically, the hot, swampy province feels like part of the new neighbouring state of South Sudan, rather than the cool highlands of the rest of

Meles Zenawi, Ethiopia's Prime Minister from 1995–2012

Ethiopia. Indeed, Gambella was effectively in Sudan when it was ruled by the British from Khartoum, until 1956. [...] Only three flights a week go to the provincial capital, also called Gambella. When you get there, there are no taxis, because there is no demand. The road from the airport is a dirt track through an empty landscape. Gambella town is a shambles. Its population of 30,000 has no waste collection system, so garbage piles up. The drains don't work, public water supplies are sporadic and electricity is occasional. There are few public latrines. The couple of paved roads are heavily potholed and give out before the town limits. My billet, the Norwegian-built guest house at the Bethel Synod church, was probably the dirtiest, bleakest and most ill-kempt building in which I have ever rested my head. The only vehicle out of town for hire was a 40-year-old Toyota minibus of dubious roadworthiness, with a crew of three. I took it.'

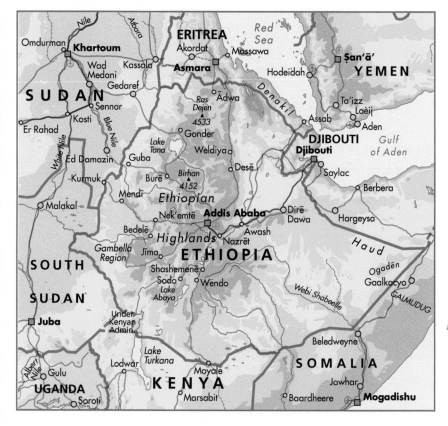

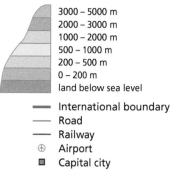

Here, countries such as Saudi Arabia and China are already growing over a million tonnes of rice a year to supply their own populations. India is also a major purchaser of land and Feza Koprucu has reported that the company Karuturi Global Ltd has developed 100,000 hectares to grow and process rice, sugar, palm oil (a biofuel) and cereals.

Narendra Modi, the current Prime Minister of India in 2014

In India, an increasing population and the trend of using more of its own farmland to produce biofuels rather than food means that the government, under the leadership of Prime Minister Narendra Modi, sees buying cheap fertile land and water resources, like rivers and lakes in poorer countries such as Ethiopia, as a solution to its food problems.

Development Indicators for Ethiopia and the United Kingdom

Indicator	Ethiopia	United Kingdom
Life expectancy (years)	42	79
Literacy rate (%)	41	99
Access to safe water (%)	27	100
Gross national product per capita ($)	100	21,410
Infant mortality rate (per 1000 live births)	110	5
People per doctor	32,000	455
Average calorie intake per adult per day	1800	3100

▶ **Consolidating your thinking** ◀

How does the data above help us to begin to understand why the government of Ethiopia could see the selling or leasing of its land to overseas countries such as Saudi Arabia as an attractive idea? Think about what a poor country needs in order to improve the living conditions of its people in places such as Gambella.

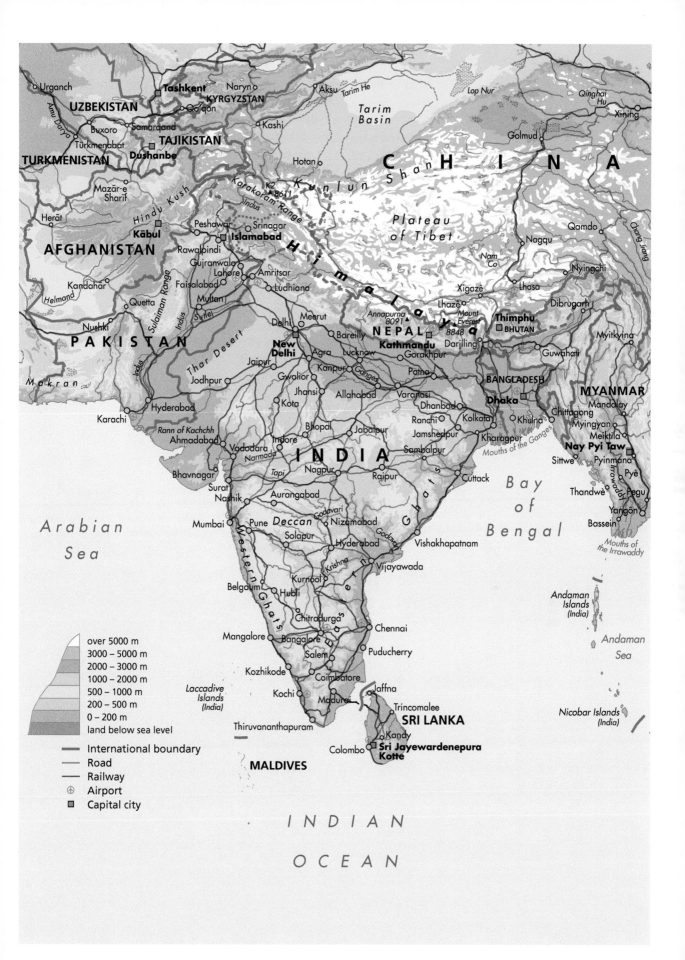

Land grabbing is economic **colonialism** and just as bad as the colonial **empires** of the past and has massive human and environmental impacts. ▶▶

Land grabbing is a very controversial geographical issue with strong opposing views as to its effect on people in the countries in which it occurs, such as Ethiopia. On 20 May 2012, Fred Pearce wrote an article for *The Observer*'s online newspaper entitled 'Land grabbers: Africa's hidden revolution'. These are two of the ninety-three comments that formed part of the resulting online discussion:

'They are called 'land-grabbers' precisely because all over Africa they are grabbing huge swathes of land knowing perfectly well what the result will be. [...] The result is people forcibly evicted from land they have farmed for generations and fertile ground used to feed foreign countries or used for other commodities that return nothing to those locals. [...] They end up with contracts that give them the land for peanuts for generations. Alongside this they extract local water resources and the local people are left not only without grazing and crop land but also water. [...] Who-ever said colonialism has ended?'

For the past forty years Ethiopia has not succeeded in feeding its population. Within another forty years the population will be three times larger with 280 million inhabitants in 2050. ►►►

'A billion people on the planet are chronically hungry, 15,000 children under five die of malnourishment each day according to the UN FAO and global agricultural output will have to increase by 50% by 2050 just to stand still because of rising populations. Anyone who thinks that Ethiopian peasant subsistence farmers are the solution is frankly mad. The only solution is technology, mechanisation, irrigation schemes and bringing vast swathes of underperforming land up to European standards of productivity. Three cheers for the land grabbers – they are the ones who are going to feed your grandchildren.'

▶ Consolidating your thinking ◀

As you can tell, people's views on the Africa land grabbing issue are *polarised* – this means that some opinions are strongly against whilst others are very much supportive. In the Teacher Book (pp.64–65) there is a set of information cards on land grabbing in Africa which provide you with a sense of what people are saying about land grabbing and the arguments they give either for or against. Working with a partner, read and sort this information into potential benefits and potential disadvantages or 'costs'. Take time to ask questions about anything you don't yet understand; for example, vocabulary used or where places mentioned are located in Africa.

Now join up with another pair and compare your two sets of cards. What similarities and differences are there? Were there any cards that contained information which was difficult to categorise as an advantage or a cost? During feedback and discussion with the whole group, take time to ask questions to help you clarify things.

Assessment piece using discursive writing

As a final task for this enquiry you are going to prepare and write a piece of **discursive writing** about the issue of land grabbing in Africa. Discursive writing aims to present a balanced argument, usually about a controversial issue, and often answers a question. Its main objective is to help people understand the different viewpoints that exist around an issue. Because so much of the study of geography is about issues, it is a form of writing that is important for you to be good at.

Your discursive piece of writing will need:

- **A title**: What are the costs and benefits of land grabbing in Africa?

- **An introductory paragraph,** in which you provide the background to the issue of land grabbing in Africa and also capture the reader's attention, encouraging them to read on.

- **A main body** of alternate paragraphs showing different sides of the argument with each paragraph introduced by a topic sentence, for example 'The arguments put forward by those who oppose land grabbing include potential social, economic and environmental costs' or 'Those who support land in Africa being sold or leased to foreign companies and countries feel that it can be a major boost to developing poorer countries'. Use the information you sorted out in the cards to form the basis of these paragraphs.

- **A conclusion,** which summarises the arguments on both sides and gives the writer's own view and recommendations.

In the Teacher Book (p.61) there is detailed guidance on how to write discursively at both *sentence* and *word* level which includes many examples of connectives that you could use in your own piece. Also in the Teacher Book (pp.62–63) is a model of a discursive piece of writing entitled *'What should happen to Amazonia?'*. You can use this to refer to as you draft and create your own writing about land grabbing in Africa. As this piece of writing is geographical, you are free to include a limited number of relevant maps, illustrations, quotations and statistics, but be sure that they are always helping rather than confusing the audience to understand the contrasting points of view that exist around this controversial twenty-first-century issue.

> In discursive pieces, the writer is free to contribute their ideas and recommendations and maybe also offer a solution. ▶▶

> In order to help a discursive piece of writing to flow as one continuous narrative, despite being made up of different arguments, you will need to use *linking words and phrases* effectively. Such *connectives* can be used both at the beginning of paragraphs and also to link ideas within a paragraph. ▶▶

7 Olympic spirit

Where should the 2022 Winter Olympics be held?

During February and March 2014, Sochi, a Russian city on the Black Sea coast, hosted the XXII **Winter Olympic Games**. Nearly 3000 athletes from eighty-eight nations participated in fifteen different disciplines. These included a range of skiing and snowboarding events as well as curling, ice skating, skeleton and bobsleigh. The hosts, Russia, topped the medal table but it was also a very successful event for Team GB as they had their most successful Winter Olympics since 1924 with one gold (Lizzy Yarnold won the women's skeleton bob), one silver and two bronze medals.

The hosts for the 2018 Winter Olympics were decided at a meeting of the **International Olympic Committee (IOC)** in July 2011, with Pyeongchang in South Korea winning at their third attempt, having previously been beaten by Vancouver (hosts in 2010) and Sochi. This time they beat Annecy, France and Munich, Germany in the first round of voting, securing sixty-three votes to Munich's twenty-five and Annecy's seven.

7.1 What factors are important in deciding who will host the Winter Olympics?

Have a look at:

http://news.
nationalgeographic.com/
news/2014/02/140214-
snow-conditions-melt-
sochi-olympics/

which describes some
of the problems that a
relatively warm climate
can bring to winter
sports and how these
can be combatted.

The IOC take a number of different factors into account when deciding upon who will have the honour of hosting the Winter Olympics. Think about what these factors might be and write a list. Try to get between five and ten factors on your list. Now rank these in order of importance with the factor you think is most important as number one.

Some countries have hosted the Winter Olympics on more than one occasion or have already hosted a Summer Olympics but not a Winter Olympics. You can see these countries on the map. Do you think that being a previous host is an advantage or a disadvantage when it comes to bidding? Why do you think this?

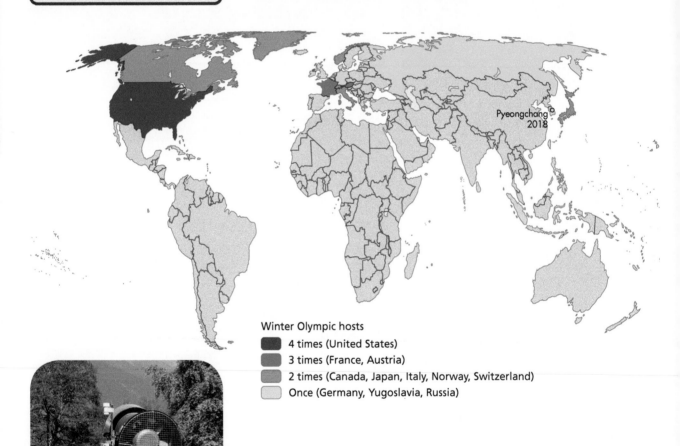

Pyeongchang
2018

Winter Olympic hosts

- 4 times (United States)
- 3 times (France, Austria)
- 2 times (Canada, Japan, Italy, Norway, Switzerland)
- Once (Germany, Yugoslavia, Russia)

Obviously, to host a Winter Olympics you need to have a climate which allows snow sports to take place. With average temperatures in February of 8.3 °C and a humid, **subtropical climate**, Sochi was the warmest city ever to host a Winter Olympics.

However, this is not the only consideration of the IOC. The host city must prove that it is large enough to be able to handle the large numbers of athletes, journalists and tourists who all need to stay in hotels and be able to travel easily to venues. The local people also need to give their support to the bid as they will be the ones who will be paying the bill...and it could be a large one! The budget for the Sochi Games was originally US$12 billion but this rocketed to US$51 billion, making it the most expensive Olympics ever.

Have a look at this infographic which highlights all of the things that had to be constructed for the Sochi Winter Olympics to take place:

http://inhabitat.com/?attachment_id=616105

Which aspect of this infographic is most surprising?

▶ Consolidating your thinking ◀

If the costs of hosting the Winter Olympics are so high, what advantages does being the successful bid bring? Create a mind map which identifies the benefits of hosting a Winter Olympics. Now, try to categorise your points by colour coding your mind map. You could think about which benefits are **social**, **political**, **environmental** or **economic**. You could think about which benefits are likely to be short term and which are likely to be long term. You could also think about whether the benefits are likely to be felt locally, nationally or globally.

Lviv

7.2 So who is in the running for 2022?

The bidding process for the XXIV Winter Olympics, to be held in 2022, is underway and there are currently five cities in the running.

They are:

- Krakow, Poland

- Oslo, Norway

- Almaty, Kazakhstan

- Lviv, Ukraine

- Beijing, China

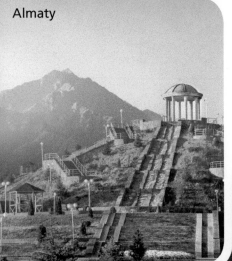

Almaty

You may have heard of some of these cities already. With a partner, discuss what you already know about these five cities or the countries in which they are located. Do you have a favourite?

Krakow

▶ Consolidating your thinking ◀

You are going to carry out a decision-making exercise to decide which of the five cities on the shortlist should be given the honour of hosting the 2022 Winter Olympics. You can use the sheets in the Teacher Book (pp.68–71) to help you to structure your enquiry.

Was the city that you chose using the ranking system the same as the city you chose at the beginning of the enquiry? Has everyone in the class chosen the same city or have people come to different conclusions? Why do you think this is? ▶▶

Beijing

Oslo

The five potential hosts

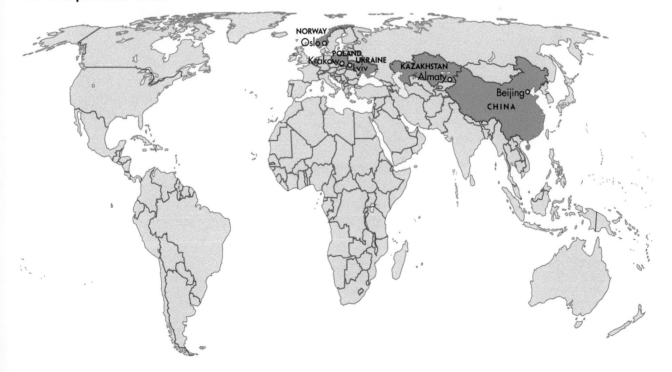

Having made a decision about which of the five cities should host the Winter Olympics you could create a website home page, welcoming people to the city. Use the activity sheet on page 72 of the Teacher Book to help you.

You are now going to draft a piece of **persuasive writing** to bring all of this information together and to help you answer the key question at the beginning of the enquiry. You are going to prepare a case which argues for the city which had the lowest score in your table. Use all of your research and the ranking table on page 71 of the Teacher Book to demonstrate that you understand the geographical reasons for your choice of host city for the 2022 Winter Olympics.

Your persuasive narrative needs to have the following structure:

- **A title:** Where should the 2022 Winter Olympics be held?

- **An introductory paragraph** to set the scene and context, in this case providing background information on the Winter Olympics and the five potential host cities for 2022. You will need to consider whether you will use maps and images to help set the context.

- **A second paragraph**, which begins with a topic sentence (this introduces the reader to what the paragraph is going to be about). In this paragraph you will describe and explain the positive reasons why your chosen city should be the host. Remember, your writing needs to be persuasive so make sure you include a range of powerful words and phrases such as 'exceptional', 'excellent' and 'phenomenal'.

- **A third paragraph**, which gives some reasons why the other four cities would not be as suitable. Whilst it would be useful to suggest factors which are negative, such as poor local support, this paragraph would also benefit from a comparison of positive factors. For example, 'Whilst both cities have strong support from the local population, the local support for city x is decreasing whilst the support for city y is increasing'.

- **A concluding paragraph**, which is a summary of the main points and answers the question. Once again, look to apply appropriate connectives such as 'in conclusion', 'in summary', 'to sum up', 'overall', 'on the whole', 'in short', 'in brief', 'to conclude' and 'so, to round off'.

Be sure to use appropriate subject vocabulary throughout your narrative, e.g. 'tourism', 'GDP', 'climate', 'local opinion', etc.

An example of persuasive writing is available for you to print off from page 73 of the Teacher Book. Read through this example carefully and highlight in green those sentences which are persuasive and well-structured. Then highlight in red the sentences which could be improved. Overall, do you think this is a successful piece of persuasive writing? Why or why not? How could it be improved? Draft new sections of narrative for those parts of the text that you feel need to be revised.

Santiago

Extending your enquiry »

7.3 Could a city in the southern hemisphere host the Winter Olympics?

One thing that is clearly missing from the Winter Olympics is a host city located in the southern **hemisphere**. The staging of the Games in February coincides with the height of summer south of the equator, therefore the climate is not really suitable. However, with new technologies making the generation of artificial snow easier to achieve on a large scale, the first southern hemisphere Winter Olympics may become a reality in 2026. There are three potential places which could mount a serious challenge: Santiago, Chile; Bariloche, Argentina; and South Island, New Zealand.

Bariloche

South Island

Southern hemisphere contenders

Select one of the three cities and design a poster to publicise a potential future Winter Olympics bid. You will need to have a logo, a motto or slogan and to select at least three reasons why this place would be a good choice of location.

▶▶
Read these three articles which tell the stories of ski resorts around the world and highlight the challenges which they face as global temperatures rise:

http://www.telegraph.co.uk/earth/earthnews/3342553/Climate-change-threat-to-alpine-ski-resorts.html

http://www.outsideonline.com/outdoor-adventure/the-current/footprint/Three-Major-Ski-Resort-CEOs-Talk-Climate-Change.html

http://www.nytimes.com/2012/12/13/us/climate-change-threatens-ski-industrys-livelihood.html?_r=0
◀◀

Having too warm a climate during the ski season is not just a problem for the southern hemisphere. The impact of climate change on **glaciated areas** is likely to be a significant feature of all regions in the future. Estimates suggest that since the mid-1980s there has been a 10% reduction in the amount of snowfall, which is likely to be due to warming global temperatures. Also, snow is likely to melt earlier in the year, which means that resorts may have to reduce the length of their seasons. The places that are likely to be hardest hit are those resorts at fairly low **altitudes**; one alternative is to move the resorts up the mountains but this is likely to have negative effects on an already vulnerable environment.

▶ Consolidating your thinking ◀

If you were the **CEO** of one of these ski resorts, what would you do? Make a list of all the things you would need to consider. Which of these do you have some control over? Which do you have little control over? Can you formulate a plan to keep the ski resort running? What would you prioritise?

7.5 Why is sustainability the key?

Just as changes in temperature will likely have a significant impact on the ability of ski resorts to generate enough income, equally ski resorts can have a significant impact on the surrounding environment. The large, heavy machinery installed to house chairlifts or gondolas creates visual and noise pollution and snow machines can deplete natural water sources in order to create artificial snow. In addition, as ski runs and pistes are developed and added to a resort, so the **species diversity** and richness of trees, flowers and birds decreases.

The Olympics has had mixed success regarding its environmental impact. Greenpeace were highly critical of the 2004 Summer Olympics held in Athens and were particularly critical that **renewable** forms of energy were not used, especially given that the city had the potential to generate vast amounts of **solar** energy. Conversely, Sydney in 2000 was cited as the first 'green' Olympics, whilst London 2012 has been held up as a positive example of how winning a bid can transform an area for the better.

► Consolidating your thinking ◄

So, with these two points in mind, how **sustainable** has the Sochi Winter Olympics been?

Are the conclusions and the messages conveyed in the documents and articles in the side panel the same? Which sources do you think are the most reliable? Why do you think this? Give the Sochi Winter Olympics a score out of ten (with ten being very environmentally sustainable). Justify the score you have given.

Finally, write a list of recommendations that you would make to the 2022 host city to make their Winter Olympics as environmentally sustainable as possible.

Read the summary of the Sochi sustainability report on pages 74 and 75 of the Teacher Book and the articles below, which detail the environmental impact that the Sochi Winter Olympics is likely to have had on the environment.

http://www.time.com/2828/sochi-winter-olympics-environmental-damage/

http://www.bbc.co.uk/news/world-europe-26152047

http://www.dw.de/olympic-winter-games-have-damaging-effect-on-sochis-environment/a-17449525

Glossary

A

acid rain rain that contains a high concentration of chemical pollutants, notably sulphur and nitrogen oxides

adaptation the process by which living organisms, including humans, change the way they live to survive better in an environment

altitude the height of anything above sea level

appropriate technology technology that is suitable to the social and economic conditions of the geographic area in which it is to be applied, is environmentally sustainable and promotes self-sufficiency

aquifer permeable rock that can hold groundwater

Armageddon a catastrophic event, especially one seen as likely to destroy the world or the human race

arid having little or no rain; too dry or barren to support vegetation

asteroid a large, irregularly shaped object in space that orbits the Sun

atmosphere the air which surrounds the earth consisting of three layers: the troposphere, mesosphere and ionosphere

B

biodiversity the variety of plant and animal life in the world or in a particular habitat

biofuel any fuel made from renewable biological resources such as plant biomass or animal waste

C

carbon emission the release of carbon dioxide and monoxide into the atmosphere

carbonate outcrop rocks made from carbonate minerals such as dolomite and limestone that are visible on the surface

Carboniferous a geological time period extending from 359 to 299 million years ago

cavern a large underground cave

CEO stands for 'Chief Executive Officer' and is typically the most senior person in a business

chalk a white, soft sedimentary rock formed from the skeletons of ancient sea creatures

climate the average atmospheric weather conditions of a place over at least a thirty year period

climate change changes in the earth's weather, especially the increase in the temperature of the earth's atmosphere that is caused by the increase of particular gases, especially carbon dioxide

colonialism the policy or practice of acquiring full or partial political control over another country, occupying it with settlers, and exploiting it economically

colony a country or area under the full or partial political control of another country and occupied by settlers from that country

commercial any activity or enterprise established with the intention of making a financial profit

condominium a building containing a number of individually owned apartments or houses

continental drift the theory that the earth's continents move slowly over a layer of liquid molten rock beneath the earth's crust

crude oil (or petroleum) is any naturally occurring flammable mixture of hydrocarbons found in geologic formations, such as rock strata

D

development indicator a numerical measure used to assess the quality of life in a country and to compare it with conditions in other countries

dolomite a sedimentary rock formed from the mineral dolomite that contains calcium and magnesium and often also iron

drought a long period of unusually low rainfall that can lead to a shortage of water

E

earthquake a movement or tremor of the earth's crust associated with plate boundaries especially subduction zones

Glossary

economy the production and consumption of goods and services and the supply of money within a country

economic benefits the financial or monetary value of something

empire a group of countries or regions that are controlled by one ruler or government

energy power, especially heat and light, obtained from physical or chemical resources

energy mix the range of energy sources a country uses to meet its power needs

environmental benefits the advantages gained from something from the natural world

Environmental Management Plan a site or project plan which ensures that any negative impact on the environment is minimised

environmental refugee someone displaced from their home as a consequence of changes to patterns of weather and climate

ethanol an alcohol obtained from sugars and starches and used as an additive or replacement for petroleum fuels

F

fossil fuels a natural fuel such as coal or gas, formed in the geological past from the remains of living organisms

G

geology the study of the origin, history and structure of the earth

geophysicist someone who studies the earth using gravity, magnetic, electrical, and seismic methods

glaciated areas places that are, or were once, covered with ice sheets and glaciers

greenhouse gases a gas such as carbon dioxide that contributes to the greenhouse effect and global warming by absorbing infrared radiation

gross domestic product (GDP) the total value of all goods and services produced domestically by a nation during a year

groundwater water held underground in the spaces between particles or cracks in rocks

H

hemisphere half of the earth usually divided into 'northern' and 'southern' by the equator and into 'eastern' and 'western' by the prime meridian

humid climate a climate that is warm and moist and usually found in tropical areas

hurricane a storm with strong winds of over 118 km/h (74 mph) that forms over warm, humid oceans

hydraulic liquid moving in a confined space under pressure

I

igneous rock formed as molten rock cools and hardens

infrastructure the basic make up of an area including, for example, roads, railways, schools, power and water supplies and drainage systems

insurance where a company provides compensation for potential loss, damage, illness or death in return for a payment called a premium

International Olympic Committee (IOC) the organisation established in 1894 with the purpose of organising both the Summer and Winter Olympic Games

L

land reclamation the process of creating new land from oceans, seas, riverbeds, or lakes

land use natural- and human-created areas of the earth's surface

lease to rent out land, property or service to an individual or company for a fixed period of time

limestone a hard sedimentary rock formed mainly from calcium carbonate or dolomite

Glossary

M

megalopolis a chain of cities which have merged together to create a continuous urban area with a population exceeding ten million

metamorphic rock rock that has been altered over time by pressure and heat

metropolitan area a densely populated major city together with its less populated surrounding areas which depend on it economically and socially

microbe a microscopic organism, such as a bacterium or virus

migration the movement of people or animals involving a permanent or semi-permanent change of residence

N

natural hazard the possibility of a natural event occurring which might cause death and destruction to people

natural vegetation everything that grows by itself in an area as a result of climatic and soil conditions without any involvement of humans

non-renewable energy energy from a source that is depleted when used, such as coal or natural gas

P

palaeontology the science that involves the study of life that existed in former geological periods

permafrost a thick subsurface layer of soil that remains below freezing point throughout the year, occurring chiefly in polar regions

permeable a material or membrane allowing liquids or gases to pass through it

Permian a geological period of time extending from 299 to 252 million years ago

physical geography the study of all things related to the earth's surface

plantation a large farming estate in tropical and semi-tropical areas on which crops such as coffee, sugar, and tobacco are grown

polder areas of reclaimed land that were once part of the seabed in the Netherlands

political benefits the advantages gained from something by the government

population density the average number of people living in each square kilometre of an area

population distribution the overall pattern of where people are living in an area

R

raw material the natural resources supplied to industries to manufacture into processed products

recreational an activity carried out purely for the purpose of pleasure

relief the general height and shape of the landscape in an area

renewable energy power that comes from sources which aren't depleted when used, such as wind

residential relating to places in which people live and their associated services

S

sediment solid fragments of inorganic or organic material that come from the weathering of rock and are carried and deposited by wind, water, or ice

sedimentary rock rock that forms as mineral and organic materials, deposited by wind, water and ice, and gradually built up in layers

seismic waves waves of energy that travel through the earth's layers, and are a result of an earthquake, explosion, or a volcano. Geophysicists use small controlled explosions to identify under surface rock formation that potentially hold oil and gas

services a system supplying a public need, such as transport, communications, or utilities such as electricity and water

sinkhole a deep hole in the ground especially in limestone landscapes, which is caused by slightly acidic rain water dissolving the rock on the surface

Glossary

social benefits the advantages gained from something by the people who live in a community or society

solar energy heat radiation from the sun converted into electricity or used directly to provide heating

solution weathering occurs when rainwater, which is slightly acidic, reacts with rocks containing calcium carbonate, causing them to slowly dissolve

species diversity the variety of living things living within an ecological community

subtropical climate the climate found mostly between 25° and 40° north and characterized by hot, humid summers and mild winters

sustainability development that meets the needs of the present without impacting negatively on the environment or compromising the ability of future generations to meet their own needs

T

tar sands a deposit of sand impregnated with bitumen, a black viscous mixture of hydrocarbons

tectonic activity the forces or conditions within the earth that cause movements of the earth's crust

tropical cyclone a very intense low-pressure wind system, forming over tropical oceans and with winds of hurricane force

typhoon a tropical storm in the region of the Indian or western Pacific oceans which generates winds greater than 118 km per hour

U

United Nations an international organization formed in 1945 to increase political and economic cooperation among member countries

V

urban a built up area such as a town or city

volcano a mountain or hill, typically conical, having a crater or vent through which lava, rock fragments, hot vapour, and gas are or have been erupted from the earth's crust

W

water table the level below which the ground is completely saturated (full of water)

Winter Olympic Games an international contest of winter sports that is held every four years

Index

Note: page numbers in **bold** refer to maps.

Index

Acknowledgements

The publishers wish to thank the following for permission to reproduce photographs, illustrations and other graphics. Every effort has been made to trace copyright holders and to obtain their permission for the use of copyright materials. The publishers will gladly receive any information enabling them to rectify any error or omission at the first opportunity.

(t = top, c = center, b = bottom, r = right, l = left)

Cover and title page image © T photography/Shutterstock.com p4 (t), p4 (tl), p4 (bl) © David Weatherly; p5 (t) © Giorgiogp2/NOAA Laboratory for Satellite Atimetry/Wikimedia Commons CC BY-SA 3.0; p5 (c) © Maciej Dakowicz/Alamy; p5 (b) © Flyver/Alamy; p6 (t) © The Official White House Photostream/Wikimedia Commons Public Domain; p6 (b) © Chipps/Flickr CC BY-NC-SA 2.0; p8 (t) © David Weatherly; p8 (c) © Sean Pavone/Shutterstock.com; p10 © Perati Komson/Shutterstock. com; p11 (t) © inoue-giro/Wikimedia Commons CC BY-SA 3.0; p11 (b) © Sean Pavone/shutterstock.com; p12 (t) © Prisma Bildagentur AG/Alamy; p12 (b) © Amy Ross/Flickr CC BY-ND 2.0; p13 (tr) © MC_Noppadol/ Shutterstock; p13 (tl) © Neale Cousland/shutterstock.com; p13 (bl) © Attila JANDI/Shutterstock.com; p13 (br) © Katherine Donaghy; p14 (t) © Pal2iyawit/Shutterstock.com; p14 (b) © JTB MEDIA CREATION, Inc./ Alamy; p14 (br) © Wikimedia Commons Public Domain; p15 (cl) © Sean Pavone/Shutterstock.com; p15 (cr) © para/Shutterstock.com; p15 (b) © LI CHAOSHU/Shutterstock.com; p16 © Anton Balazh/Shutterstock.com; p17 (t) © TOMO/Shutterstock.com; p17 (b) © David Weatherly; p18 © Ryoma35988/Wikimedia Commons CC BY-SA 3.0; p20 (t) © Universal Images Group Limited/Alamy; p20 (b) © Horizon Images/Motion/Alamy; p21 (tl) © Carpkazu/Wikimedia Commons CC BY-SA 3.0; p21 (tr) © KPG_Payless/Shutterstock.com; p21 (c) © Tooykrub/Shutterstock.com; p21 (b) © AP/Press Association Images; p22 © surassawadee/ Shutterstock.com; p23 © AndySmyStock/Alamy; p24 © Markus Mainka/ Shutterstock.com; p26 © Martin Luff/Wikimedia Commons CC BY-SA 2.0; p28 © AP/Press Association Images; p30 (t) © Alastair Rae/Flickr CC BY-SA 3.0; p30 (b) © hugo Soria/Wikimedia Commons CC BY-SA 3.0; p31 (l) © Stanford's Geological Atlas of Great Britain and Ireland edited by H. G. Woodward F.R.S. third edition 1914/Maprooms.com Public Domain; p31 (tr) © diak/Shutterstock.com; p31 (cr) © daniela kalman/ Shutterstock.com; p31 (br) © diak/Shutterstock.com; p32 (l) © Horst Gutmann/Flickr CC BY 2.0; p32 (c) © AG-PHOTOS/Shutterstock.com; p34 © ulrichstill/Wikimedia Commons CC BY-SA 2.0; p36 (t) © DonkeyHotey/ Flickr CC BY 2.0; p36 (bl) © goghy73/Shutterstock.com; p36 (b) © Christopher Stadler/Flickr CC BY 2.0; p36 (br) © AgelessVisionsPhoto/ Wikimedia Commons CC BY-SA 3.0; p37 (t) © tristan tan/Shutterstock. com; p37 (c) © Rob Hainer/Shutterstock.com; p37 (b) © Florida Geological Survey; p38 (t) © aquapix/Shutterstock.com; p38 (b) © Ian Bottle/Alamy; p41 © NOAA Geophysical Fluid Dynamics Laboratory/ Wikimedia Commons Public Domain; p42 (tl) © spirit of America/ Shutterstock.com; p43 (tr) © Tom Reichner/Shutterstock.com; p43 (cr) © Tom Reichner/Shutterstock.com; p43 (c) © Jim West/Alamy; p42 (b) © 2009 USDA Farm Service Agency/U.S. Department of Agriculture/ Google Earth; p43 (b) © 2014 Google/Google Earth; p44 (t) © Jim West/ Alamy; p45 (t) © Stephen Saks Photography/Alamy; p45 (cr) © Jim West/ Alamy; p45 (cl) © Jim West/Alamy; p45 (bl) © ZUMA Press, Inc/Alamy; p45 (br) © NASA/Earth Observatory; p52 (tl) © Steve Oehlenschlager/ Shutterstock.com; p52 (cl) © Sarah2/Shutterstock.com; p52 (b) © sigur/ Shutterstock.com; p53 © Arma banchang/Shutterstock.com; p55 (tr) © David Burr/Alamy; p55 (cr) © Kristian Buus/Alamy; p55 (br) © Cernan Elias/Alamy; p55 (b) © Randi Sokoloff/Shutterstock.com; p56 (t) © topora/Shutterstock.com; p56 (b) © Alex Mit/Shutterstock.com; p56 (br) © SSSCCC/Shutterstock.com; p57 (t) © Steve Morgan/Alamy; p57 (cl) © julius fekete/Shutterstock.com; p57 (cr) © Andrew Zarivny; p57 (bl) © majeczka/Shutterstock.com; p57 (br) © Anthony Harrison CC BY-SA 2.0; p58 (tl) © Nobu Tamura/Wikimedia Commons CC BY-SA 3.0; p58 (l) © Illustration by Bex Glover for the English Riviear Global Geopark; p58 (cr) © johnbraid/Shutterstock.com; p58 (br) © Fulcanelli/Shutterstock. com; p59 (l) © Andreas Wahra/Wikimedia Commons Public Domain; p59 (c) © Dr Chris Proctor/Torquay Museum; p60 (t) © Stocktrek Images, Inc./Alamy; p60 (br) © Dmitry Bogdanov/Wikimedia Commons CC BY 3.0; p60 (bl) © The Natural History Museum/Alamy; p61 (tl) © Artwork by Brin Edwards for the English Riviera Global Geopark; p61 (tr) © Linda Bucklin/ Shutterstock.com; p61 (b) © The Natural History Museum/Alamy; p61 (c) © Ron Blakey, NAU Geology/Wikimedia Commons CC BY-SA 3.0; p62 © English Riviera Global Geopark; p63 (cl) © English Riviera Global Geopark; p63 (cr) © Global Geoparks Network; p63 (b) © Contains Ordnance Survey data © Crown copyright and database right 2011; p64 (tl) © andrew payne/Alamy; p64 (cl) © English Riviera Global Geopark Tourism Company; p64 (cr) © English Riviera Global Geopark Tourism Company; p64 (bl) © Torquay Council Beaches Team; p64 (br) © Chris Slack Photography; p65 (c) © Stocktrek Images, Inc./Alamy; p65 (b) ©

ARCTIC IMAGES/Alamy; p66 (t) © Images Etc Ltd/Alamy; p66 (b) © Basilicofresco/Wikimedia Commons CC BY 2.0; p67 (t) © Sergio Bertino/ Shutterstock.com; p67 (b) © Catmando/Shutterstock.com; p68 © Designua/Shutterstock.com; p69 © Nipik/Wikimedia Commons Public domain; p72 (t) © Illustration by Bex Glover for the English Riviear Global Geopark; p72 (b) © David Weatherly; p73 (tl) © Nik Taylor/ Alamy; p73 (tr) © David Weatherly; p73 (c) © David Weatherly; p74 (tl) © Dona_Bozzi/Shutterstock.com; p74 (cl) © aragami12345s/ Shutterstock.com; p74 (bl) © fotostory/Shutterstock.com; p74 (br) © Charles Harker/Shutterstock.com; p75 (cl) © deamles for sale/ Shutterstock.com; p75 (cr) © africa924/Shutterstock.com; p75 (bl) © drli/ Shitterstock.com; p75 (br) © guentermanaus/Shutterstock.com; p76 (cl) © Nicholas Sheehan; p76 (cr), p76 (br), p77 (tl), p77 (cl) © EM-DAT: The OFDA/CRED International Disaster Database/www.emdat.be, Université Catholique de Louvain, Brussels (Belgium); p78 (t) © Cynthia Hunter/ FEMA News Photo/Wikimedia Commons Public Domain; p78 (b) © Barry Lewis/Alamy; p79 (t) © Capt Darin Overstreet/defenseimagery.mil/ Wikimedia Commons Public Domain; p79 (b) © Concept use/ Shutterstock.com; p80 (tl) © dave stamboulis/Alamy; p80 (tr) © Neil Cooper/Alamy; p80 (c) © Alex Proimos/Wikimedia Commons CC BY 2.0; p80 (b) © Aurora Photos/Alamy; p81 (tr) © joyfull/Shutterstock.com; p81 (c) © Caro/Alamy; p82 (tl) © Filip Bjorkman/Shutterstock.com; p82 (cl) © Paul Stringer/Shutterstock.com; p82 (bl) © HankShiffman/Shutterstock. com; p84 (c) © Remi Kaupp/Wikimedia Commons CC BY-SA 3.0; p84 (bl) © Stephen Riley/Flickr CC BY-NC-SA 2.0; p84 (br) © arindambanerjee/ Shutterstock.com; p85 (t) © glenda/Shutterstock.com; p85 (tr) © arindambanerjee/Wikimedia Commons CC BY-SA 3.0; p85 (cl) © UN Photo/ UNICEF/Marco Dormino/Flickr CC BY-NC-ND 2.0; p85 (b) © NOAA; p86 (tl) © Filip Bjorkman/Shutterstock.com; p86 (cl) © SmileStudio/Shutterstock.com; p86 (bl) © Efired/Shutterstock.com; p88 (c) © Edwin Verin/Shutterstock. com; p88 (bl) © epa european pressphoto agency b.v./Alamy; p88 (br) © NOAA; p89 (tl) © audioscience/Shutterstock.com; p89 (tr) © Lance Cpl. Marie Matarlo/U.S. Marine Corps/Wikimedia Commons Public Domain; p89 (br) © Art Phaneuf – LostArts/Shutterstock.com; p89 (bl) © saiko3p/ Shutterstock.com; p90 © Marc F. Henning/Alamy; p91 (t) © Richard Whitcombe/Shutterstock.com; p91 (c) © Richard Whitcombe/Shutterstock; p92 (tl) © Edward Linley Sambourne/Wikimedia Commons Public Domain; p92 (cr) © The Strobridge Lith Co. Cincinnati/Wikimedia Commons Public Domain; p92 (bl) © Keystone View Company/ Wikimedia Commons.com; p92 (br) © Rudolf Hellgrewe/Wikimedia Commons Public domain; p93 (c) © Carte Générale de l'Afrique, Librairie Larousse 1898-1904/Wikimedia Commons Public Domain; p93 (t) © igorGolovniov/Shutterstock.com; p93 (t) © Brian Maudsley/ Shutterstock.com; p93 (cl) © Lefteris Papaulakis/Shutterstock.com; p93 (b) © Lefteris Papaulakis/Shutterstock.com; p94 (t) © Ryan M. Bolton/ Shutterstock.com; p94 (tl) © Pierre-Yves Babelon/Shutterstock.com; p94 (c) © think4photop/Shutterstock.com; p94 (bl) © Boleslaw Kubica/ Shutterstock.com; p94 (b) © EugenZ/Shutterstock.com; p95 © eyeidea/ Shutterstock.com; p96 (t) © Federico Rostagno/Shutterstock.com; p96 (tl) © egilshay/Shutterstock.com; p96 (c) © Maridav/Shutterstock.com; p96 (bl) © Photo Image/Shutterstock.com; p96 (b) © Jim Parkin/ Shutterstock.com; p97 © Virtual Steve/Wikimedia Commons CC BY-SA 3.0; p98 (t) © TonyV3112/Shutterstock.com; p98 (br) © XiXinXing/ Shutterstock.com; p99 © TonyV3112/Shutterstock.com; p100 © Tupungato/Shutterstock.com; p102 © World Economic Forum/ Wikimedia Commons CC By-SA 2.0; p104 (tl) © Ricardo Stuckert/ Wikimedia Commons CC BY 3.0; p104 (c) © wandee007/ Shutterstock.com; p106 (t) © Oxfam East Africa/Wikimedia Commons CC BY 2.0; p106 (c) © MartinMaritz/Shutterstock.com; p106 (b) © africa924/Shutterstock.com; p107 (t) © Vlad Karavaev/Shutterstock. com; p107 (c) © Luisovalles/Wikimedia Commons CC BY 3.0; p107 (b) © Oxfam East Africa/Wikimedia Commons CC BY 2.0; p108 (t) © Brendan Howard/Shutterstock.com; p108 (c) © Lefteris Papaulakis/Shutterstock. com; p108 (bl) © PathomP/Shutterstock; p108 (br) © IRRI Images/ Wikimedia Commons CC BY 2.0; p109 © Jiri Flogel/Shutterstock.com; p110 (c) © Dainis Derics/Shutterstock.com; p110 (b) © Herbert Kratky/ Shutterstock.com; p111 (t) © Olga Popova/Shutterstock; p111 (cl) © Herbert Kratky/shutterstock.com; p111 (cr) © Martynova Anna/ Shutterstock.com; p112 © yykkaa/Shutterstock.com; p113 (tl) © yykkaa/ Shutterstock.com; p113 (bl) © Julia Kuznetsova/Shutterstock.com; p113 (tr) © ID1974/Shutterstock.com; p113 (br) © Martynova Anna/ Shutterstock.com; p114 © De Visu/Shutterstock.com; p114 (c) © Pikoso.kz/Shutterstock.com; p114 (b) © badahos/Shutterstock.com; p115 (l) © zhu difeng/Shutterstock.com; p115 (r) © joyfull/ Shutterstock.com; p117 (t) © Pablo Rogat/Shutterstock.com; p117 (c) © nicolasdecorte/Shutterstock.com; p117 (b) © wolfmaster13/ Shutterstock.com; p118 © Tatiana Popova/Shutterstock.com; p119 © ChameleonsEye/Shutterstock.com